JOY COMES IN THE MORNING
(31 stories and devotions to begin your day)

By
Joseph Akins

CONTENTS

ACKNOWLEDGEMENTS

Thanks be to God for allowing this project, for providing every resource needed, and for His faithfulness in all things.

Thanks to my family for their loving support in this project and so many other areas. (Thanks, too, for being such a great source of material!)

A special thanks to my niece, Alyssa. You probably worked even harder on this than me. You are the best, and I am not just saying that because I am your favorite uncle.

So many wonderful friends have been incredibly supportive during this process---the BCI team, the Grace family, the TPC family. Each one of you has contributed in various ways. I thank you with all my heart. Without your constant encouragement, I would not have been able to follow this dream.

To Craig Morris, Steve Weech, and Steve Buchholz---you gave me validity. There are few things more empowering than Godly men who believe in you. Thank you doesn't begin to cover my gratitude.

All glory be to God above. May His Name be praised forever and ever!

FOREWORD

It is a great honor to write the forward of this publication.
When asked to write this, I must admit, I was rather
surprised. However, I soon realized Joseph didn't know
anyone else who would say anything good about him; so
here goes. I know you will enjoy the humor and parody in
which Joseph presents a clear message of service in these
last days. His parenthetical style is amusing and hits home
without hurting (too much). I have enjoyed the journey of
this book and have had opportunity to preach some of these
entries. Each entry will inspire you to dig deeper in your
Christian walk as the common things of life prove so
important in our day to day walk with Christ. The format is
light and airy, but the message is strong and distinct. You
will laugh at everyday blunders and mishaps and see yourself
in many of the same situations. Joseph brings the Scripture
into each entry and gives us practical application of God's
Word for everyday living. My prayer is that you read this
book and receive the blood, sweat, and tears of a man who
just like us is endeavoring to serve God as we see the Day
approaching.

Craig Morris
Senior Pastor
Grace Assembly of God
Jesup, GA

INTRODUCTION

I remember the way I got started in sports reporting. I loved to write wild stories as a child (I vaguely recall something about tigers and another about a big bass called "the General"), but I had long before given that up until one day when I had a conversation with a boss. I was working part-time as an assistant football coach at my high school alma mater and one day I stopped by the school office before practice to check out the articles about our team in the local paper. As I read the minimal coverage and what I considered to be poor reporting, I casually remarked that the coverage was pitiful and that even I could do better than that. Unfortunately (or fortunately), the principal was in the office at the time. Being gifted in the art of sarcasm as I was, he shot back, "Well, if you think you can do a better job, why don't you go down to the paper and apply for a job?" My rebellious nature reared its ugly head and I said coolly, "You know, I think I will." Realizing he had struck a nerve, the principal backed off a little and said, "Well, if you really are interested, I think they have a position open." "Thanks," I replied, "I will check on it today." And I did---- embarking on a short, yet illustrious career as a sportswriter (illustrious, being in the eye of the beholder).

I started writing sports editorials in much the same way. One day I read an editorial from one of the big city papers, and thought to myself, *"You know, I think I could do this. How hard could it be?"* I worked on a piece and submitted it to my editor who thought it might work. Soon, I had a weekly column in our local paper and fancied myself as a "real" writer; but when I left my hometown, I really thought I had left writing behind as well.

I tell you this because, although I can mark the beginning of every season of writing, I really can't say how this project began. One day, I sat down at the computer and began to type some observations that were rolling around in my head. I sent this in an e-mail to a few friends, and before long I was typing out another observation. With encouragement and support from these friends, I eventually realized I was working on a book; and although I never felt this project was a directive from God, His inspiration and provision have definitely been what has made it possible. If you are looking for deep theology and exegesis of Scripture, let me offer my most humble apology. You have picked up the wrong book. However, if you like to laugh----at yourself and sometimes others; and if you have a love for God's Word and are frequently looking for Its practical application in your life, then I hope this book is for you. You are certainly who it is written for.

This may not be like any devotional or collection of writings you have ever read, but perhaps that is a good thing. Our goal is to laugh while still tackling thought provoking subjects, to enjoy humor without sacrificing a reverence for Scripture. Over the next 31 days (or 31 minutes) take a journey with me and we will look at the silly and serious sides of life. This is a journey on which laughter is solicited and exploration of the Holy Bible is encouraged, and on this journey the parenthetical reigns. Enjoy the trip.

CHAPTER 1

TORN BRITCHES

My father is a treasure trove of southern colloquialisms, particularly humorous ones. I love them and I use them anytime I think I can get away with it, but I have two problems. First, my use of any of those phrases usually seems contrived. Second, I simply can't remember all of them-----especially when it's the right time to use one. Now when my father uses them, it's a different story. He normally isn't trying to be funny and the phrases just flow in his conversation. I guess that's what makes them "colloquialisms", huh? I try to work a phrase like "as regular as a three-legged dog hops" into a conversation, but I just don't seem to have his knack for it.

Of all the ones I have heard through the years, by far my favorite is the one he dropped on me when I was in early adolescence. "Well, I guess I tore my britches with him," he said. Tore his britches??? I wasn't aware that my father had been climbing any barb wire fences with a friend. What exactly did tearing of the britches entail? (No pun intended by the way!) Well, the formal definition of "tearing one's britches" with another is as follows: The party of the first part has not made a favorable impression upon the party of the second part and a parting of ways has occurred. Apparently, if you offend, anger, or, in general, tick off another person to the degree that amends aren't likely to be made, you have "torn your britches with them." (I think there is also the connotation that you have exposed a certain part of your anatomy in the process, but my father would never elaborate on that part.)

In any case, I have always been amused by the phrase. I still use it occasionally, but it usually elicits raised eyebrows----- not that this is a problem for me, mind you. I just prefer to be understood if I am going to bother with speaking. But, as I am prone to do, I recently started contemplating the spiritual ramifications of some of my favorite sayings and I made an amazing discovery concerning this one. People have been tearing their britches for thousands of years! That's right. In Jesus' time they probably said something like "I just rent my robe with him", but the meaning was the same---the party of the first part was not getting along with the party of the second part.

Conflicts are nothing new. You donl't need me to tell you that. We can look at a newspaper or the television at any time to see the residual of age old conflicts in the Middle East, or anywhere else for that matter. And if foreign affairs aren't enough, we can look in our own country, state, or city to see the havoc conflict wreaks. Perhaps we need only go as far as our community or next door or even.....well, let's just say that we have all experienced conflict close to home. The problem with conflict is that it always, every time, without fail leaves a scar. Anyone who has ever *literally* torn their britches knows that once a garment is torn, it is ruined. Never again can those britches be considered your "good jeans". Now they are "work jeans" or maybe even worse---"rags".

Conflict has lasting effects and nobody in history was any more familiar with that fact than David. David is easily my favorite Bible character. Most of us David fans like to think of him as that "man after God's own heart", but David had some conflict issues going on. He had conflict with his brothers, with his boss, in his love life, with his children…and we haven't even gotten to his enemies yet! David had a gold star in conflict and each one of them left some kind of mark on him. However, there is one story that is particularly interesting to me -- the story of David and Shimei.

Shimei is the man from Saul's tribe, the tribe of Benjamin, who curses David in 1 Samuel 16. David has become king, replacing Saul, but is now running for his life from his own son, Absalom, who is attempting to usurp his throne. The Scripture says Shimei came out to meet David *"….cursing continually as he came."*(KJV) He even threw stones at David and his men. Now, where I come from, that means somebody's got some "torn britches". I don't know exactly whose britches were torn with whom, but there was a huge rip somewhere.

You can read the account in chapter 16, but the bottom line is that, at this point, David chose not to retaliate. You can also read in chapter 19 of 1Samuel that when David returned that way, victorious and vindicated, Shimei ran out to meet him singing a different tune. Though spurred on by his men to take his vengeance on Shimei for his prior transgressions,

David again chose not to retaliate. He continues on to be restored as king and it seems as if this is the end of the story---except for one thing. David never forgot Shimei. Though Shimei tried his *darnedest* to mend the tear (think about it) he could not repair the damage that had been done. The words that had gone out could never be retrieved; and Shimei's best tailoring job would still leave a seam, a scar that would always stay with David.

Now, fast forward to the end of David's life---the deathbed scene. For his entire life, David had chosen not to take revenge on Shimei. However, listen to his instructions to Solomon. 1Kings 2:9 *"But now, do not consider him (Shimei) innocent. You are a man of wisdom; you will know what to do to him. Bring his gray head down to the grave in blood."* Wow. There are eight verses of instructions that David gives Solomon. There are two that refer to serving God. The remaining six deal with how Solomon should reward certain people based on how they treated David during his life. In essence, David said, "Be strong. Be a man. Walk in the way of the Lord and keep his commandments so that you succeed at whatever you do. Now, let's get down to some unfinished business."

There's a little more to it than that, but not much. David had three people in mind that he wanted paid back for their deeds and/or words and two of them were not good. This man after God's own heart spent the last few precious moments of his life giving three times as much instruction about payback as he did about following God. I'm not knocking David. Remember, I'm a David fan, but this story is an awesome picture of the scars that words and deeds can leave. Have you ever found yourself running your finger over a repaired hole in an old pair of jeans you're wearing? Something about that rough edge draws us to it and we will often unconsciously smooth it down with a thumb or forefinger, periodically rubbing it as if when can smooth it away. I see David doing that to the scar on his heart----ever so often running a spiritual finger over the mended place, but never able to smooth away the damage.

Oh, that we would see the lasting effects of our words and actions----the damage we can do to others…..and the damage we can do to ourselves. Shimei's words left a mark on David, yes, but they ultimately cost *him* his own life. 1Kings 2:46a *"Then the king gave the order to Benaiah son of Jehoiada, and he went out and struck Shimei down and killed him."* Every loose word we speak is not going to come back to kill us, but we really don't know what damage it will do ultimately, do we? The good news is that positive words and deeds work in the same fashion. David carried the scars of his conflicts to his grave, but he also carried fond memories of a man who befriended him in the most difficult hour of his life. The power of life and death truly is in the tongue.

There is one last thing that must be said and I know some of you have been chomping at the bit (I worked another one in) to set me straight on this. Jesus can give us a brand new heart, and He can heal all the wounds of our past. He specializes in the impossible, so I never want to imply that anything is beyond his "fixin". However, our charge is to never cause the kind of damage that Jesus has to come in and fix. It has been said that people are like elevators---we are either taking people up or we are taking people down. Which one are you doing?

CHAPTER 2

JUST THE FACTS, MA'AM

A man was taking a stroll through the park on a beautiful Spring day and passed by another gentleman resting peacefully on a park bench. Beside the man was a handsome Rottweiler tied to a lamppost.
"Does your dog bite?" asked the first man.
"No, not at all," replied the seated gentleman.
So, the man out for a stroll stepped off the path and extended his hand to give the beautiful dog a pat on the top of the head. Suddenly, the dog lunged at the man with a snarl and a snap, causing the man to fall backwards. Escaping with all his appendages intact, the man was still livid and literally screamed at the seated gentleman.
"I thought you said your dog doesn't bite!"
"That's not my dog," replied the man.

In the old TV show, "Dragnet", Jack Webb's character, Sgt. Joe Friday, was famous for a one-liner he faithfully delivered anytime a witness began to ramble. "Just the facts, Ma'am," Joe would say. (Of course, it didn't work very well with the male witnesses, but I digress.) The man who wanted to pet the dog would have been better served if he had gotten *all* the facts. Usually we call the minute facts "details"; and details can be easily overlooked. Unfortunately, it's these overlooked little facts that can get us into trouble.

Naturally, it's the men that have the most trouble with this. We don't want to ask for directions and we don't want to read the instructions. We would rather sit up all Christmas Eve with parts scattered around us than to admit that we need a piece of paper to tell us how a bicycle fits together. There's no doubt in my mind that it was an exasperated wife who coined the phrase, "When all else fails, read the instructions." Many times, we find ourselves in difficult situations because we don't know the details; but often we find ourselves in trouble because we ignore them.

One day, I was cutting wisteria out of a pine tree that was growing beside the driveway. I wanted to cut the vines as high up the tree as I could reach, but I only had a step ladder to use. I made a bad mistake at the onset when I decided to use the step ladder improperly. I knew that step ladders are designed to be opened up and used with all four legs on level ground, but I decided to lean the closed ladder against the tree instead. My second mistake was even bigger. When I approached the step that bore the warning "Don't step on or above this step," I decided that this, obviously, did not apply to me. As I stood upon the very top of the ladder extending my clippers high above my head, I discovered that the warning, in fact, did apply to me.

The ladder went one way and I almost went the other. I say "almost" because, in a desperate attempt at self-preservation, I wrapped both arms around the pine tree. I would like to tell you that I hung there momentarily and then shimmied down the tree unscathed or that the fire department came and rescued me. I would like to tell you that, but I can't. Neither of these things happened. Instead, I slid down the tree, shelling bark off of it like it was a corn cob in an old timey corn sheller. Have you ever seen one of those cartoons where a character slides down a roof and shingles fly right and left as he falls? You get the picture. Fortunately, I landed with a thud 6 inches to the correct side of the driveway; or I would have had a cracked skull to go along with my raspberried arms, stomach, and chin.

Details matter. Instructions matter. And God is particularly adamant about us following His. David found this out early in his reign when he decided to bring the Ark of the Covenant to the city of Jerusalem. In 1Chronicles 13 we read how David made plans to retrieve the ark. Mosaic Law commanded that the ark be transported on poles on the shoulders of the Levites, the tribe of priests. Instead, David had the ark transported on an ox cart driven by two men named Uzzah and Ahio from the tribe of Benjamin. I don't know if the fact that the two came from the same tribe as Saul had anything to do with David's decision, and I don't know why he chose an ox cart. In his zeal, perhaps David thought a cart would get the ark to Jerusalem faster. I find it interesting that he used a "new" cart. Was this supposed to appease God in some fashion? "I know we aren't following your instructions, but this is a *new* cart." Maybe David thought it would make things better, or maybe he just wasn't paying attention to the details…but God was. *v.9, 10 - 9 When they came to the threshing floor of Kidon, Uzzah reached out his hand to steady the ark, because the oxen stumbled. 10 The Lord's anger burned against Uzzah, and he struck him down because he had put his hand on the ark. So he died there before God.*

David was upset by God's actions; and I must admit, when I was a young boy, I too thought God was being a big meanie here. I didn't understand why God would strike poor Uzzah down when he was trying to do a good thing. After all, did God want him to just let the ark hit the ground? If we aren't supposed to let the flag touch the ground, how much more important would the Ark of the Covenant be? It took me a while to understand how serious God is about following his instructions. It took David and Uzzah just a split second.

1Chronicles 14 tells the story of two battles David had with the Philistines. I don't think it is a coincidence the writer goes into detail on how David sought God and followed His directions exactly. It is even more evident that David learned his lesson in chapter 15 when he decided again to bring the ark to Jerusalem. This time, he acknowledged his error and did things according to God's instruction. That endeavor ended in celebration. What a lesson! When we do things our way, the result is death. When we follow God's plan, we have a celebration in the end. Just a few details, but they make all the difference in the world.

CHAPTER 3

IF GOD CAN USE BALAAM'S ASS.........

My chocolate lab is probably the most talkative dog I have ever seen. Of course, it's in doggie language with all sorts of unintelligible, guttural noises; but as my niece would say, "Sometimes I think he's going to break out in English!" Often, when we are riding along in the pick-up truck, he will cock his head to the side and give me some contemplative look which I am certain means, "I have something important to tell you." But each time I respond to the "look" with my standard "What?" response, he can only respond in excited whines and barks.

It's a shame that we can't verbally communicate. After all, we're big friends. And for those of you who don't believe that a dog is man's best friend, try this experiment: lock your dog and your wife in the trunk of your car, come back in one hour, open the trunk, and find out who is *really* glad to see you. *Disclaimer: That was a* **joke**. *Do* **not**, *under any circumstances, attempt the aforementioned experiment.*

The point is, try as they may, our pets cannot verbally communicate with us. We would love them to and are so intrigued with the idea that we even entertain ourselves with talking animals in movies and television characters like "Mr. Ed" (ask your parents---they will explain). We enjoy the fantasy, but we know that in reality this could never happen…or could it?

Numbers 22 tells the story of Balaam, a man who knew he was called to BE a prophet, but couldn't overcome his desire to make a profit. Read the story and you will find how Balaam appeared to be doing the right things but all along was looking for a way to advance his will instead of God's. The story culminates with Balaam's ass, hereafter referred to as "Donkey", saving him from destruction by stopping in the road and refusing to pass by an angel poised to strike Balaam dead.

Oblivious to the danger, Balaam responded to Donkey's efforts by beating her with a stick three times. Being extremely patient, as most animals are, Donkey took the first two beatings without complaint; but upon the third attack, the Lord opened her mouth and Donkey said, *"What have I done to you, that you have struck me these three times?"* That's right---Donkey just started talking plain as day. It gets better. When Donkey posed her question, Balaam didn't die on the spot from a massive coronary; he ANSWERED her. Now, we have all asked our pets questions as if they could understand and even as if they were supposed to answer. But can you imagine what you would do if Fluffy actually did answer. "What am *I* doing drinking out of the toilet? Why did *you* leave the toilet seat up?" Such a conversation would cause more than one cardiac arrest, but not with old Balaam;

he just jumped right into the dialogue.

v.29 "Then Balaam said to the donkey, 'Because you have made a mockery out of me! If there had been a sword in my hand, I would have killed you by now. '" Poor Balaam. He thought Donkey was trying to make a donkey out of him! We still haven't gotten to the best part. Because Balaam still couldn't get his focus off himself, Donkey began to *reason* with him... *v30 "The donkey said to Balaam, 'Am I not your donkey on which you have ridden all your life to this day? Have I ever been accustomed to do so to you?"* Of course, Balaam had to respond, "No." Can't you just hear Balaam saying, "Well, I never thought of it that way before. Since you put it like that, I guess I was pretty silly." How can you read this chapter without laughing out loud?

The account of Balaam's journey continues on, but I want to focus on Donkey's part in the story. I have often mused that a wonderful sermon title for this portion of scripture would be "If God Can Use Balaam's Ass, He Can Use You Too," but to my knowledge, no one has jumped on that gem. Still the question begs to be answered: What does it take to be used by God? There are many answers to that question that can be gleaned from scripture, but are there any pointers we can pick up from Donkey?

First, she was faithful and consistent. Remember what she pointed out to Balaam? *"Am I not your donkey on which you have ridden* all your life to this day?*"* Donkey had put in a lot of years of service, and they were probably years of rather menial labor. Still, she did it until that day without grumbling and without ever opening her mouth. Now, there is a lesson for you! Don't be discouraged in the lowly tasks or the years of seemingly unnoticed service. God sees all, knows all, and you never know----there may be a special task He has waiting ahead designed just for your unique talents.

Secondly, Donkey was perseverant. She knew what had to be done, and she would not be forced or prodded to do otherwise. She even endured physical beating and still refused to concede. Sure, you could say that she was simply acting on survival instinct and was avoiding the angel with the drawn sword to save her own hide, but so what? Maybe if Balaam had viewed obedience to God as a life or death situation, he would have avoided much of his trouble. Perhaps we all need Donkey's kind of "survival instincts".

Thirdly, she had vision. Balaam was supposed to be a prophet, yet he could not see what was plain to a donkey. Donkey did not have her own agenda. She was not blinded by ambition, pride, or a promise of wealth. She was focused on her job and thus had perfect vision regarding the things that mattered most at that moment.

There you have it. If you have the attributes of a donkey, you can be used by God. Don't be discouraged if you haven't attained some lofty station that someone told you was "real" service. Don't seek position; seek purpose. Never give up. Galatians 6:9 says, *"Let us not lose heart in doing good, for in due time we will reap if we do not grow weary."* And remember, if God can use Balaam's ass.........

CHAPTER 4

YOU WANT ME TO DO WHAT????

Once a man slipped from a cliff and nearly plunged to his death, saved only by desperately grabbing a shrub growing out from the cliff's sheer rock face. All alone, suspended hundreds of feet above jagged rocks and in obvious terror, the man cried out to God for help. He begged and pleaded, promising the rest of his days to dedicated service if God would just answer and save him. Then, when he thought he could hold on no longer, he heard the sweetest sound he had ever heard.

"You called?"

"God, is that you?" the man cried.

"It's me. Do you trust me?"

"Yes, yes, yes Lord," the man shouted, "I trust you. I trust you more than   anything."

"Then let go of the shrub."

"W...W...What???" the man stammered.

"Let go of the shrub. Let go and I will catch you.

(Silence)

"Well?" the voice called.

With renewed vigor, the man yelled back, "Is anyone

ELSE up there?"

Hopefully, you haven't had to dangle off the side of a cliff, but chances are you have had some sort of experience where the action of your faith was a lot more difficult than the discussion of it. Following God's direction can be relatively simple when it fits neatly into our preconceived ideas, but when He asks us to step out of our comfort zone we suddenly feel the need to "consult" with God to make sure He knows what He is doing. "Well, it sounds pretty good from your end Lord, but let's just take another look at exactly what you are asking from me."

Of course, in most cases, we don't just come out and argue with God. Our reluctance is usually in the form of "needing a sign" or "time to counsel with other brothers or sisters". And there is absolutely nothing wrong with that...unless it hinders you from doing what you already *know* God has told you to do. Still, even when we "know it in our knower", sometimes God asks us to do some things that are way beyond our comprehension. That is when true faith gets to exercise.

We find one of those stories in Acts 9: 1-13. Saul (soon to be renamed, Paul) is fresh off of his participation in the murder of Stephen and is now sweeping the countryside in search of any believers he can take captive to Jerusalem. Saul is cruel and ruthless. Furthermore, his notoriety for persecuting the followers of Christ is known by everyone, certainly by every believer. On the road to Damascus Saul has his own encounter with God, but let's fast forward to v.10 where the Lord speaks to a man called Ananias.

Ananias has an awesome story. It is told in just a few verses, but the little we read speaks volumes about faith. The Lord comes to Ananias in a vision and calls him by name. There is nothing necessarily unusual about that because, obviously, God knows us all by name. However, this is where I am first impressed with Ananias. He answers immediately by saying, "*Behold, here am I, Lord.*" Three things catch my attention here. Ananias is quick to answer, he recognizes the voice of the Lord, and he is available. That's not a bad place to start. It's always a good thing to be familiar with the Master's voice and when He speaks we want to be ready and willing to act. It seems Ananias was willing until…

The Lord gave Ananias a very simple command. Well, it was simple in the sense that it was detailed. I mean, Ananias even had the address of where he was supposed to go for goodness' sake.

"Ananias, I need you to do something for me."

"Sure, Lord, my pleasure."

"I want you to get up."

"Check."

"I want you to go to Straight Street"

"Check."

"I want you to go to the house of Judas"

"Check."

"And I want you to pray for a man there named Saul of Tarsus."

"You want me to do WHAT?!?!?!"

Well, three out of four ain't bad. But it is, isn't it? With God it is all or nothing and Ananias knew this. So, as most of us would, he decided to get "clarification".

"Lord, I know you have probably been really busy lately and you might not have the whole story on this Saul guy. Now, *I*

29

hear that he's been causing a *lot* of trouble for your people, Lord----- even killing folks. And it's not just me saying that, Lord. Everybody has been talking about it. Now, are You sure it was Saul of *Tarsus* you wanted me to pray for?" Okay, it didn't go quite that way, but you get the picture. Ananias needs to make sure he understood what God wanted him to do.

To bring it into perspective, imagine this conversation.

"Joseph, I need you to do something for me."

"Sure, Lord, my pleasure."

"I want you to go to Pakistan."

"Check."

"I want you to meet a man named Achmed at the airport."

"Check"

"I want you to travel 50 miles out of the city with him to a cave in the mountains."

"Check."

"And I want you to pray for a man there named Osama Bin Laden."

"You want me to do WHAT?!?!?"

If that conversation ever takes place you had better believe Joseph is getting "clarification".

The fact is we don't really know for sure what was going through the mind of Ananias. It is easy to make assumptions based on what we think we might have done. He is pegged as the "unwilling servant" and we assume he was scared spitless, but let's take a closer look. He makes himself available to God. Nothing wrong with that. He dialogues with God and expresses concern over what appears to be an unusual request by God. Nothing really wrong with that. He followed the directions to the letter without delay. Definitely nothing wrong with that.

There is one last aspect of the story and, to me, it is the most important. Sure, Ananias might have needed "clarification", but, ultimately, not only did he obey the command of the Lord----he *embraced* it. I don't know how long the trip to Straight Street took, but in the time it took to get from his house to Judas' house, he had gone from viewing Saul as an enemy to viewing him as a brother (v.17). Not only did he help him, he accepted him. Talk about real faith in action!

There are a lot of examples in Scripture of dialogues between God and man, so I don't really think he minds our questions. I do know he minds our disobedience. With that in mind, I pray whenever we are faced with the difficult tasks of life, we will always come down on the side of complete and faithful obedience. Above all, I pray we will have faith like Ananias and learn to embrace the seemingly unachievable. With our God, all things are possible.

CHAPTER 5

THAT VOODOO THAT YOU DO

I think Simon the Sorcerer gets a bad rap. I mean, by the time we meet him in Acts 8:9 he has already given up the "craft" and is even described as "a certain man named Simon, who *formerly* was practicing magic in the city" (my emphasis added). Yet, even though he is a believer when we're introduced, we still tag him with a label from his past. That just doesn't seem right. How would we like to be known that way?

"There goes Tommy the Thief." "Here comes Gabby the Gossip." "Hi, I would like to introduce you to Larry the Liar."

The point remains that we want to forget our transgressions 10 seconds after they occur, but poor Simon is labeled for all posterity by his past. Now, part of this is certainly due to that fact that, even though he is a believer when we meet him, he still has not gotten his act together. There is no reason to believe that his salvation experience was not real. Phillip was convinced enough to baptize him. (I'm assuming that Phillip did his own baptizing.) v.13 *"And even Simon himself believed; and after being baptized, he continued on with Philip; and as he observed signs and great miracles taking place, he was constantly amazed."*

Simon sounds like one of those guys who gets saved at a big revival meeting and then doesn't miss another service while the evangelist is in town. I can just see him on the front row waving a hanky and shouting, "Amen!" And his sitting on the front row might have been what got him into trouble. By the time Peter and John got to town in v. 15, Simon was probably already gaining some position in the church. He was most likely ushering or collecting offerings and may have been up for the next Sunday School teaching position. Obviously, I don't know what was going on with Simon, because Scripture doesn't say, but I am pretty sure he had to go through some huge changes.

You see, we do know Simon was very accustomed to being in the limelight. His use of the black arts had given him fame and everyone had given him attention saying, *"This man is the divine power known as the Great Power."* (v.10) Of course, when the people saw the true "Power of God", Simon's exploits were forgotten-----to everyone except Simon. Again, I don't know, but I would guess that Simon had a hard time giving up all that attention, the obvious wealth that was tied to his craft, and of course, the power. He believed, certainly, and he was as amazed as everyone else by the awesome power of God; but sometimes old habits are hard to break.

Perhaps, the breaking point for Simon was when Peter and John arrived in town and began to pray for people to receive the Holy Spirit. When Simon saw them laying hands on people and witnessed the signs and wonders that followed this new experience, maybe he thought, "This is my ticket back. This is how I can have the best of both worlds." So, he offers to pay for the authority of conveying the Holy Spirit. I like to imagine him introducing himself to Peter and John, "Hi Guys, my name is Simon---you've probably heard of me" (uncomfortable silence). "No? Well, you probably didn't realize it, but I have a little experience in this field myself."

When he gets around to making his offer, Peter lets him have it with both barrels. The first reaction is to think this is just Peter being Peter----brash, loud, and a bit over the top. However, since the advent of the Holy Spirit, this isn't the same old rough fisherman. He is operating in new gifts and you have to believe he had a better feel for what was going on than we do. And since it is detailed in Scripture, it is safe to conclude that Simon had some heart issues to correct. However, here is where I think Simon gets the bad rap. He is vilified for attempting to buy authority, but I see a new convert who stumbled a little, or perhaps a lot, on his past (*Maybe* because everyone kept calling him Simon *the Sorcerer*!).

The reason I am taking Simon's side here is because of his reaction to Peter. Instead of being indignant, he was repentant. A lot of people who had been dressed down like that would have responded, "How dare you!!", "Do you know who I am?", or my personal favorite, "The Bible says 'Judge not that ye be not judged'." Simon didn't come back with any of that. V.24 *"But Simon answered and said, 'Pray to the Lord for me yourselves, so that nothing of what you have said may come upon me."* When Peter told him to pray, Simon, in effect said, "I thought I had, but obviously I'm missing something. You guys pray for me so I get it right."

That one verse tells me that Simon should forever lose the "Sorcerer" title. He wasn't perfect and he had a lot of growing to do, but by submitting to Peter and John he showed humility. And, by submitting he rejected the sin that makes many of us more of a sorcerer than Simon. Huh? That's right. When we are rebellious, God equates us to witches and sorcerers. 1st Samuel 15:23 – *For rebellion is as the sin of witchcraft, and stubbornness is as iniquity and idolatry. Because thou hast rejected the word of the LORD, he hath also rejected thee from being king.*
That is strong stuff, but God is serious about our submission to His authority. Thankfully, He is also serious about forgiveness and renewal. So, if you have been practicing your own form of witchcraft, give it up like Simon did and submit to God's authority. And just be glad we don't have to wear our past on our nametag like he did. Nobody wants to hear "Look, here comes Steve the Sorcerer."

CHAPTER 6

SLAVE OR BOND-SERVANT

There once was a wife of an avid deer hunter who decided that a good way to spend more "quality" time with her husband would be to take up hunting. Her surprised, yet somewhat pleased, husband consented to the request thinking no possible harm could come of his wife tagging along to the woods. Early the next morning, the man placed his wife in one of his favorite tree-stands with all the proper instruction and the assurance that if and when she fired on a deer, he would be close by and come running to assist. Just as he started to climb his own stand he heard the familiar report of the gun he had placed in his wife's hands only moments earlier. Blam!........Blam! Blam! He raced back to where he had left his wife and found her with her gun drawn on a poor man in hunting attire, his hands raised over his head and sweat beginning to bead his brow. "Honey, what in the world is going on?" the husband exclaimed. "This is my deer," she announced, "This is my deer and he's trying to take it." "Yes ma'am, it's your deer," the frightened man stammered, "It's definitely your deer...just let me get my saddle off of him and you can have him!"

That little story is just another way of saying you can call something whatever you want, but it doesn't change what it is. Changing the name doesn't change the substance. It seems like we spend a lot of time trying to dress up things. We dress up ourselves, our cars, our homes. Hey, we'll even dress up our pets, but the one thing most of us will always dress up is our image. We might consider being a sanitation engineer, but we would never be a janitor. I, myself, am no longer a balding, fat guy approaching middle age. Instead, I am now a folically impaired man with increased experience who happens to be gravitationally challenged. Whatever you do, don't call us by a title that would demean our dignity.

Unfortunately, this pride of life is also a spiritual attitude. Don't call us *slaves* to Christ, because we are *bond-servants*. Well, I've got news for you brother/sister......IT'S THE SAME THING! That's right--dust off that Strong's Concordance or pull out your Webster's and you will find that slave and bond-servant have the same definition. "Well, that can't be! A slave is pressed into service against his/her will under horrible conditions. God wouldn't want me to be a slave. He wants me to offer my service cheerfully." Of course He does, but not because HE needs it. YOU need to serve cheerfully. The people who are trapped in this mindset are the same ones who think that they found Jesus. Let me let you in on another secret. Jesus wasn't lost----we were. And because He found us, we owe Him the greatest debt that can never be repaid by mere servitude. It deserves, no, it demands the complete and total transfer of our lives to Him.

The problem is we are kind of hung up on that whole "free will" thing. "Okay....you're right...I do have to sell out to

God completely, but I am *choosing* to do it and I know that after I pull my time here on earth I'm going reap my great heavenly reward." We reconcile the servant/slave issue by becoming indentured servants. You remember the concept. If your ancestors came to this country in the 1600 – 1700's there is 50% chance you descended from indentured servants---poor people who sold *themselves* into slavery for period of time (usually 3-7 years) to gain some sort of social advantage or reward, normally money or land. It was actually based on the Hebrew law found in Deuteronomy 15 and for a period of time was a popular way for poor Europeans to get to this country. This plan sounds better to us, because it is our idea and we still have our freedom of choice.

If that helps you get your mind around it, great. In fact, we do have choices. We just aren't the totally autonomous beings we like to think we are. We live our day to day lives thinking we are in complete control of the choices we make. Especially here in the good ol' US of A, the land of the free, we have lulled ourselves into this blind arrogance that we don't have to do anything (except pay taxes) that we don't want to do. Don't get me wrong. I love my country, and I thank God everyday for the liberties we enjoy here. However, the temporary freedoms we enjoy in the physical realm have absolutely nothing to do with who we serve in the spiritual realm. What we fail to understand is that our choice is not about whether or not we will be a slave, but rather about whose slave we will be.

Matt. 6:24 tells us we can only serve one Master and Peter breaks the slave issue down even more in 2Peter 2:19 – *".....for a man is a slave to whatever has mastered him."*

38

For goodness sakes people, even Bob Dylan gets it---
"You're gonna have ta suuuuve somebody." Come to the
realization that you are a slave----either you are a slave to sin
or you are a slave to God.

So what am I trying to do---tell you a funny story and then
hit you between the eyes with the fact that you are destined
to a life of slavery? Well, I do have a bit of sadistic streak,
but actually I come bringing good news. Once we realize
that becoming a slave to Christ is our reasonable service and
we wholeheartedly commit to Him (this is where that whole
cheerful thing kicks in), we suddenly discover what true
freedom is all about. That's right; the only way to know true
freedom - freedom from sin - is to become a slave to Christ.
Don't take my word for it. Paul says it perfectly in Romans
6: 17,18,22,23 -- *17 But thanks be to God that, though you
used to be slaves to sin, you wholeheartedly obeyed the form
of teaching to which you were entrusted. 18 You have been
set free from sin and have become slaves to righteousness.
22 But now that you have been set free from sin and have
become slaves to God, the benefit you reap leads to holiness,
and the result is eternal life. 23 For the wages of sin is death,
but the gift of God is eternal life in Christ Jesus our Lord.*
Are you really satisfied being just a servant? Do you want to
be truly free? Then become a slave to the right Master. His
yoke is easy and His burden is light.

CHAPTER 7

A LITTLE REMINDER

"Watch where you put your feet, Son," my father cautioned
again. I had heard that instruction at least a million times in
my life. (Of course, I'm exaggerating---I'm sure it wasn't
more than a few thousand.) Anytime that I had wandered
into grass that reached my ankles, I heard my father's
warning: "Watch where you put your feet, Son."
Sometimes, I would get the instruction as I left the house,
before I even approached a blade of grass. Sometimes, it
would come after I had waded into a potentially dangerous
area, but it always came. It was like clockwork. And here
we were again. An 82 year old man giving his 44 year old
son basic instructions as we cleaned up around an old shelter
on the farm. I had to smile as my mind went back to one of
those warnings I received about 15 years prior.

I love blackberry jelly and learned years ago from my
mother how to make it. The only real difficult part is
gathering the fruit. Blackberries are small and it takes quite a
few to produce a significant amount of jelly (and a
significant amount of jelly is all I'm really interested in!).
However, the biggest problem with gathering the berries is
the blackberry bush itself. It is laden with briars and usually

grows in the wild in grassy, weedy areas. Several years ago on my father's farm, a large number of blackberry bushes had volunteered in an old, unused garden patch. Other than the high grass around them, the blackberries were in an ideal spot to be easily picked and I couldn't wait to get a bucket of them.

This old garden spot even had a road that encircled it, so my father putted along beside me in his old truck and talked to me as I gathered the berries. Naturally, though I was a grown man, my father had to render the admonition he had given me for years, "Watch where you put your feet, Son." Now at this point of my life, I was pretty independent and certainly didn't think I needed to be reminded of what I had been taught since childhood. Besides, thanks largely to that teaching, I had avoided many a rattlesnake in my lifetime and was acutely aware of the hazardous area I was treading. I decided to inform my father of that little fact. "I know, Daddy," I said, "I am watc...." and before I could complete the word, a covey of quail flew up in my face. Amidst a flurry of flapping wings and loose feathers, I let out a scream that sounded like a girl encountering a mouse in her sleeping bag, as I high stepped it out of there with my kneecaps up around my ears. Few things are more startling than having quail fly in your face while thinking about rattlesnakes at your feet.

The one positive out of the experience was I had never seen my father laugh that hard in my life. When he finally gained his composure, he called out, "Did that scare you, Son?" I informed him that, in fact, it did scare me and asked him if he would give me a ride back to the house so I could "freshen up".

I'm sure my father has given me deep advice and instruction over the years, but none has served me better than, "Watch where you put your feet, Son." When I was inclined to go places I knew better than to be, I heard that warning in my ears, "Watch where you put your feet, Son." When I was heading down a path with the wrong set of friends, I could hear it. When I was about to jump, feet first, into the wrong situation, it rang in my ears. This simple little warning has served me well through the years; but as simple as it is, there have been many times that I forgot it or didn't put it into practice.

Do you suppose my father repeated it to me so many times through the years because he thought I was too dense to catch the concept? (Careful!) No, he did it for two reasons. One was that my life was too precious to him for him to be concerned about whether or not my intelligence would be insulted. The risk of embarrassing, annoying, or insulting me held no weight compared to my safety. The second reason was my father knew everyone needs a little reminder occasionally, no matter how simple the concept might be.

It is interesting to me that Paul, Peter, and John used the same "little reminder" philosophy in their writings long before my father ever thought of it. All three of these biblical patriarchs addressed the use of repetitive teaching in their writings.

1 Corinthians 15:1 -- *Now, brothers, I want to remind you of the gospel I preached to you, which you received and on which you have taken your stand.*

42

1 Peter 1: 12-15 -- *12 So I will always remind you of these things, even though you know them and are firmly established in the truth you now have. 13 I think it is right to refresh your memory as long as I live in the tent of this body, 14 because I know that I will soon put it aside, as our Lord Jesus Christ has made clear to me. 15 And I will make every effort to see that after my departure you will always be able to remember these things.*

1 John 2:7 -- *Brethren, I write no new commandment unto you, but an old commandment which ye had from the beginning. The old commandment is the word which ye have heard from the beginning.*

I often hear people who have held a Christian faith for many years express a desire for a "meaty" teaching. They want to be intellectually stimulated; but while it is true Paul talked about progressing from the "milk of the word", we see that he never intended for us to forget foundation principles. Beyond that, too many of us desire to move on when we really haven't mastered the basic tenets of our faith.

It reminds me of the pastor who tried out for a new church and preached the best message the congregation had ever heard. They enthusiastically voted him in 100% and the next Sunday the new pastor assumed his duties and preached the exact same message. The congregation thought little of it. Perhaps, the pastor didn't have time to prepare another message in the midst of his move and besides, it *was* a great message. However, when the pastor preached the same message on the third Sunday, eyebrows were raised. On the fourth Sunday, when he preached it again, an emergency meeting was called and the head of the deacon board posed the question on everyone's mind, "Why don't you preach another message?" The pastor calmly replied, "When you start acting on the first one, I will."

My father expressed his concern for my welfare with repeated warnings. Our heavenly Father does the same thing. Whether we are the one who still needs to put the basics into practice or whether we are the one who needs the little reminder to check the foundation periodically, God faithfully and gently guides us back to safety through the repetition of His Word. So, the next time you're annoyed because you find yourself on a path that seems a little too familiar, remember---we all need a little reminder.

CHAPTER 8

CAN YOU HEAR ME NOW?

While on one of my semi-weekly visits to the redneck mall (hereafter referred to as Wal-Mart), my pleasant shopping experience was interrupted by the piercing shriek of a child. Initially thinking the child was injured, my heart brimmed with sympathy. "Poor child, he must be in tremendous pain." The shrieks continued. "Poor parents, losing a child at such a tender age -- and in Wal-Mart, no less." The shrieks continued.

At some point it dawned on me that these were not the screams of a poor child in agony, but rather the tantrum of a young lad who had been crossed by a hapless parent. (I say hapless because the parent(s) obviously had not enjoyed the benefit of the Henry Akins School of Child Rearing which my father unofficially ran for years.) Since I enjoy working with children and may have the opportunity to do so again, I will not put into print my initial reaction when I discovered little Johnny was throwing a fit. Let's just say I was, well, slightly agitated. I was slightly agitated, but I was extremely curious. I had to get a look at this kid who could single handedly shut down a Super Wal-Mart.

I quickly grabbed my merchandise and followed my ears toward ground zero. It didn't take long to cross paths with a frazzled lady ushering little Johnny toward the front entrance. Hmmph. He didn't look like a terrorist. A shade over 3'6", freckles, average build…wait a minute…he did have a sort of renegade look in his eyes. Still, I was thinking the lady could take him in two out of three falls. I couldn't catch the whole gist of the young man's grievance, but it was obvious he was not in a cooperating mood.

I couldn't help but recall some of my own childhood experiences. For some reason, I thought of an elderly woman who introduced herself to me years ago by saying, "I remember your brother when he was 'pinched on the bench'." "Pinched on the bench" referred to a technique my father practiced on my siblings and perfected on me some time later. If we ever got a case of the wiggles in church, a quick glance and nod of the head would summon us to come sit on the pew beside our father. If that was not enough to stop our fidgetiness, with fingers like a skilled violinist our father would take a small plug of our outer thigh between his thumb and forefinger and apply vise like pressure. By using this technique, he could render you instantly motionless or make you sing the national anthem. Resistance was futile. We quickly learned that compliance lessened the pressure and resistance increased it. I'm no rocket scientist, but I got the lesson down pat in the first 6 seconds the technique was used on me.

As I meandered my way back to reality, I realized that such "strong arm" tactics were archaic; but I certainly hoped that little Johnny was heading for time out. Still, as I looked around the store and noticed virtually everyone speaking in hushed whispers and pointing, I had to hand it to the kid---he was no quitter. He knew what he wanted and he was not going to be deterred. I didn't necessarily agree with Johnny's application of the virtue, but it can be a good quality to have. Bartimaeus certainly thought so.

Bartimaeus was the blind man we find in Mark 10 begging on the roadside near the gates of Jericho. When he heard that Jesus was passing by he shouted out, "Jesus, son of David, have mercy on me!" In fact, he yelled it more than once. I wonder if Jesus heard Him the first time. From Scripture it appears that they were in close proximity to each other. If Jesus has the ability to feel virtue exit the hem of his garment, then certainly He can hear someone yelling His name. Yet Bartimaeus received no response. Being blind and not having the benefit of a mobile phone network, Bartimaeus reached out and touched someone the only way he knew how. He yelled all the louder, "Son of David, have mercy on me!"

This time Jesus stopped. Mark 10:49, 50 - *49 Jesus stopped and said, "Call him." So they called to the blind man, "Cheer up! On your feet! He's calling you." 50 Throwing his cloak aside, he jumped to his feet and came to Jesus.* Isn't it interesting that Jesus didn't say, "Go get him" or "Bring him here"? Of all the people who would qualify for assistance to get to Jesus, a blind beggar sounds like a prime candidate. However, just like the rest of us, Bartimaeus had to come to Jesus on his own accord. Apparently, this wasn't a problem as he leapt to his feet and, I imagine, ran to Jesus. He was convinced that if anyone could help him it would be this Jesus of Nazareth....and Jesus did not disappoint. But then again, He never does.

Are you convinced that Jesus is the only one that can help you? If you are, are you willing to do whatever it takes to reach Him? The woman with the issue of blood was. Bartimaeus was. If I were God (let's all thank Him I'm not), I would be a little spoiled by that. I would have a hard time answering people who half-heartedly called my name when there were so many seeking me with everything they had. Yet God, in His divine nature, does not think like that. He is eternally merciful and faithful....even when we are not. Life offers many trials and tribulations, but Christ always offers hope. He offers life and He offers peace. What a motivation to seek Him with our whole heart.

When I left Wal-Mart, I could still hear little Johnny screaming in the parking lot. "Wow," I thought, "That little guy isn't going to give up." I don't really think that was what Jesus was talking about when He said we need to be like little children, but who knows? We've already established He doesn't think like we do. The next time you feel like giving up, remember Johnny. Call out to Jesus and let your voice be heard. He can hear you now...and always.

CHAPTER 9

EVERYBODY NEEDS A JONATHAN

Once, the Lone Ranger and Tonto were galloping west across the prairie when they spied an approaching band of Indians in the distance. The Lone Ranger turned to his trusted compadre, Tonto, and asked, "What do we do now, Tonto?" "We go east, Kimosabi," came Tonto's swift reply. Heading east the duo soon came upon another band of Indians approaching in the distance. "What do we do now, Tonto?" the Lone Ranger again asked. Without hesitation came the answer, "We go north, Kimosabi." After only a few minutes on the new trail, another band of Indians was spotted in the distance. Again came the question, "What do we do now, Tonto?" Back came the obvious response, "We go south, Kimosabi." Heading south, the pair soon saw the rising dust of yet another band of Indians. Frantically, the Lone Ranger cried out, "What do we do *NOW*, Tonto?" Again the reply was swift. "What do you mean *WE*, Paleface?" Tonto shouted as he broke into an Indian war cry.

Unfortunately, most of us have experienced that kind of friendship somewhere in our past. It's that friend who promises to be there for you, but in your hour of need is nowhere to be found. It comes in varying degrees. It might be the guy you helped move who is suspiciously missing when it's time for your move or it could be the gal that you babysat for who promised faithfully to return the favor and is now not returning any of your phone calls. It could be something serious. Perhaps, you have felt the pain of betrayal by someone you trusted with an intimate detail. No matter our history, the disappointments we endure help us appreciate the true value of friendship whenever we find it.

David was no different. In fact, in his lifetime, he felt the sting of rejection in just about every relationship you could imagine. It started with his father in 1Samuel 16 when Samuel came to Jesse's house by the Lord's direction to anoint a new king as Saul's replacement. Jesse sent seven of his sons by Samuel and didn't even consider David for the selection process. It's tough when your own father doesn't believe in you. David could have adopted some kind of complex right there and sought out therapy or a talk show host to help him blame his father for his anxiety disorder. Instead, he accepted the anointing by Samuel and the Spirit of the Lord came upon David from that day forward. This was a good thing, because David was just beginning a long pattern of relational disappointments.

The next one came quickly. We all know the story of David and Goliath in 1Samuel 17, but we often gloss over the chilly reception David received from his oldest brother, Eliab, when he got to the battlefield. David was obeying his father's instructions and doing a favor for his three oldest brothers, but Eliab became angry with him and attacked his motives. Maybe Eliab was jealous, because his baby brother had been chosen over him for kingship. Maybe he was weary from battle. Whatever the reason, David was let down by another family member. We know the rest of the story. David was not deterred, again rose to the occasion, and defeated Goliath. That earned him a job with the king, but even that relationship went south in a hurry.

In 1 Samuel 18, we find that David's boss (Saul) tried to kill him with a javelin...not once, but twice! I have had some rough days at work, but I have yet to have an employer make an attempt on my life. Talk about a severance package. Still, the stories continue. David's wife, Michal, scorned and rejected him when he danced before the ark; and his son, Absalom, rebelled against him and tried to take his kingdom. Let's face it. David knew a little bit about being disappointed in a relationship, but David had one thing that everybody needs---he had a Jonathan. (Well, actually, he had *the* Jonathan, but work with me here.)

Jonathan is also introduced in 1 Samuel 18 and verse 1 tells us that Jonathan loved David "as his own soul". That's a lot of love where I come from. Most of us are familiar with the story of David and Jonathan's amazing friendship and I won't attempt to retell it here. If you need to refresh your memory of their story, it's woven beautifully in the pages of I Samuel. By now, you've probably thought of a Jonathan in your life. I hope that you have one. I know that I do and you're probably waiting on me to tell some story about how he pulled me out of a burning building or something. Well, he's never had to do that, but he has always made me feel like he would if it were necessary. But, this isn't about my Jonathan...or yours either. "What are you talking about then? I thought you said everybody needs a Jonathan?"

They do, and that is why *YOU* need to be one.

I don't know if you played Lone Ranger and Tonto when you were a child, but everybody wanted to be the Lone Ranger. Do you ever remember anybody volunteering to be Tonto? "Come on, Jim. You played Tonto last time. It's my turn now." I don't think so. Nobody wants to be the sidekick. Everybody's a Batman; nobody's a Robin. Everybody wants to be David, but nobody wants to be Jonathan. The fact is we all like to be loved and served, but how willing are we to give sacrificial service? That means service that costs time, sweat, emotion, resources, or, quite probably, some combination of them all; and it's all done without a press conference.

As Christians, we are called to follow Christ's example and what better picture of self-sacrifice could we have? It is such a priority to Him that the only way we can achieve greatness in His kingdom is to humble ourselves in service. Your mother was right when she told you, "If you want friends, you're going to have to show that you are a friend." If you want to have a Jonathan, you first need to learn to be a Jonathan.

We probably don't need to be reminded about how awesome the Jonathans in our lives are. Maybe we do need to be reminded that we should be a Jonathan for them. If you *have* taken your Jonathan for granted, returning their sacrificial love is a wonderful way to say thank you. After all, everybody needs a Jonathan. Are you meeting someone's need?

CHAPTER 10

DON'T BE SANDY
(UNLESS THAT'S YOUR NAME)

I love the beach, but I'm not really what you would call a "beach person". I love the sun, the surf, the clean, salt air----in fact, for me the only problem with the beach is.....THE SAND. I know, I know, the beach IS sand. (Well, technically, it's not, but I'm not here to split hairs.) My point is that I have an issue with sand.

How can I say I love the beach and then say I have an issue with sand? Well, it's really not all that odd. I enjoy playing in the sand. I like to feel it between my toes and it can be beautiful to see, but why does it have to get into EVERYTHING? I don't hate sand. I just want it to stay at the beach. I will be glad to come and visit it on occasion, but I don't want to take it home with me and make it a house guest.

Anybody who has been to the beach knows what I'm talking about. Soldiers who have served in the desert know it as well. If you are on the sand, the sand is going to get on you.....and in you....and in your stuff.....and in any crack and crevice whether you think it's exposed or not. In fact, it

can even find its ways into supposedly sealed containers.
Let's face it---it's just insidious stuff.

Of course, not everyone shares my point of view. There are
those who walk right past those conveniently place showers
at the beach, hop into their cars, and head home never caring
that they have half of a sand castle attached to their legs.
Worse yet are those people who will plop down on the beach
to sun themselves without the benefit of a towel or a beach
blanket. They just lie there and wallow in the sand like it's
suntan lotion. Whenever I see those guys, I just laugh to
myself because I know that in just a little while they are
going to find out firsthand about the whole "crack and
crevice" thing.

Why does any of this matter? It doesn't really, but it
correlates conveniently to a similar spiritual condition. On
our brief visit here on earth (remember we are not of this
world), we tend to get a little too much "earth" on us. This is
a problem. Because just like our mother who told us,
"You're not coming into my house until you get that dirt off
of you!" God says we can't come into *His* house unless we
are clean of the world's attachments. When we accept God's
gift of salvation, we are changed, become new creatures, and
are promised a heavenly home, but this doesn't mean that
our new lives are maintenance free.

Jesus gave the perfect explanation when Peter protested the
Master washing the feet of the disciples, specifically his.
John 13:10 -- *Jesus answered, "A person who has had a bath
needs only to wash his feet; his whole body is clean. And you
are clean, though not every one of you."* In the second part
of the verse Jesus refers to the impending betrayal by Judas,

but in the first line He makes it perfectly clear that after the initial cleansing of salvation we are still required to keep the dirt of the world from lingering on our spiritual bodies. We may not need a total cleansing, but spot removals are necessary.

The problem with the world is it can be just like that infernal sand. Little remnants of it like to cling to you even after you think you've removed it from every area of your life. And don't even mention those cracks and crevices. How many times has a little "world" slipped out in our seemingly pious lives, leaving us to question, "Where did that come from?" This is not a message of fear. I don't propose that we hide in some sterile church environment to avoid getting the grime of the world on our white suits. On the contrary, we are commanded to GO into the world and preach and make disciples no less. We just have to be conscious that while we are in the world, the world will constantly be trying to get back into us. This means we have to maintain our Christian walk.

It *doesn't* mean we have to run to the altar and get saved every time the pastor gives an altar call, like some may suggest. On the other hand, we can't walk the aisle when we're 12 and expect that we never have any maintenance to do over the next 70 years, as others seem to think. Just look at it like a young couple in love walking on that sandy beach. You know the ones. They slip off their shoes and roll up their pants legs and wander hand in hand along the shoreline occasionally dipping their feet into the shallow tides. They may stroll for hours, but what happens when they return to their car? They have sand all over their feet! Now when they pass by those conveniently placed showers at the beach, they stop and rinse their feet before they slip on their shoes. They don't stand under the shower head and take another shower. That isn't necessary. Their bodies are clean (this was a big date for goodness sake---they had a bath before they left the house) and their garments are clean (spotless maybe?) so all they need to do is wash the areas that came in contact with the beach.

The concept is simple and the process is simple, but it is also simple to overlook. Jesus washed the disciples' feet because they needed it and because He wanted to teach them to have the heart of a servant, but He knew this was a perfect way to teach them a great doctrinal lesson at the same time. He deemed it important and we should as well. Don't let the simplicity of the process cause you to overlook the importance of the issue. Leave it to Jesus to teach a philosophy of life, a tenet of doctrine, and get the menial work done all in one fell swoop. As for us, let's not neglect our call to the world. Just remember---don't be sandy!

I SEEEEE YOU

It was final exam day for the large university English class and the professor gave the final instructions: "You have exactly one hour to finish the exam. At the end of that time all test papers must be turned in finished or not." As the hour came to a close, papers began to trickle in. Soon the professor said, "Time"; and all the remaining students brought their exams and laid them in a neat stack on his desk before filing out of the room----all the students but one.

One young man remained at his desk, furiously scribbling on his test paper.
"Time has expired, young man," the professor said. "It's time to turn in your exam."
The young student ignored the professor and continued to work on his test.
"Young man," the professor said a little irately, "You must turn in your test immediately."
Nothing.
"That's it, Sir," the professor announced, now considerably agitated. "If you do not bring that paper to my desk this instant, I will not accept it."
The young man did not even look up and for ten more

minutes continued to work on the test. Finally, with a completed exam in hand, the student approached the professor's desk.

"I'm sorry, young man, but I told you I would not accept that paper," the professor smugly informed him.

"But, Sir," the student replied, "You don't know who I am do you?"

"It doesn't matter who you are," the professor retorted, "I'm not accepting that paper."

The young man persisted, "But do you know who I am? The professor nearly exploded, "I don't care if you are the son of the university president. I am not accepting that paper."

"So, you don't know who I am?" the student asked again. The professor finally caved. "No, Son, I don't. I don't know who you are."

"Good," the young man said grinning; and he stuffed his paper into the middle of the stack and dashed out of the room.

Sometimes anonymity can be good. We have all experienced some embarrassing moment in a store or some other public place and walked away thinking, "I'm glad no one here knows me." Or maybe we weren't so lucky and we *wished* no one there knew us, as we stood there all red-faced wanting to crawl under a rock. But it doesn't have to be an embarrassing situation. Whether it is insecurity or a survival instinct, there is something in our human nature that makes us all want to hide at one point or another.

The daughters of my good friends love to play hide and seek, but one of their absolute favorite things to do is to hide in a room and jump out to scare you whenever you enter.

Sometimes they just like to hide in the room to make you wonder where they are. Usually there are lots of giggles and occasionally a foot or arm sticks out from under the table, but we play along anyway. "Where could those girls be?" Anyone with kids has played that game. It's almost as fun for the adults because we are so amused at how they think we can't see them since they can't see us. Do you think God gets amused with us in much the same way? "Those silly humans. Do they really think that I can't see them?"

Adam and Eve were the first to play hide and seek with God. Gen 3:8, 9 - *8 Then the man and his wife heard the sound of the Lord God as he was walking in the garden in the cool of the day, and they hid from the Lord God among the trees of the garden. 9 But the Lord God called to the man, "Where are you?"* Maybe we learned how to play along with the game from God himself. "Where are you?" Do you really think God didn't know exactly where they were? Did they think he didn't know?

They were the first, but they certainly weren't the last. Their son, Cain, took it up a notch by trying to hide his brother's dead body and thus his own sin. (I make my own assumptions on hiding the body since this is not specifically stated in Scripture.) Moses did the same thing with an Egyptian; but prior to that, as a baby he was hidden by his parents in the bulrushes. Rahab hid the spies; Gideon hid from the Midianites; David hid from Saul; Elijah hid from Jezebel; and the prophets hid in caves. The list is seemingly endless; but whether the subjects were hiding from God, a physical enemy, or simply hiding their talents, every story has one thing in common: God saw it all.

There is nothing that escapes the eye of our God. He is all-seeing and all-knowing. That can be an extremely comforting thought when we are in distress or face difficult trials, but it is an equally discomforting thought when we stray into areas we know we should have avoided. We have no anonymity with God. David said in Psalm 139:13 - *For you created my inmost being; you knit me together in my mother's womb.* Now that is being known. He knows our innermost parts and He knows our innermost thoughts. How could we ever hide anything from Him? Yet we still try. Why do we think that we can hide things from God?

Perhaps part of the answer can be found in 1Cor 2:7 - *No, we speak of God's secret wisdom, a wisdom that has been hidden and that God destined for our glory before time began.* and 1Cor 2:11 - *For who among men knows the thoughts of a man except the man's spirit within him? In the same way no one knows the thoughts of God except the Spirit of God.* It would seem that God does a little hiding too. No, He doesn't deliberately try to hide like we occasionally do. It's His very nature which is spiritual in essence and too awesome for us to ascertain that makes Him such a mystery that He might as well be hiding.

The good news is the mystery can be revealed by His Spirit who searches all things, even the deep things of God (1Cor 2:10). When we trade earthly wisdom for spiritual wisdom and adopt the mind of Christ, our vision becomes supernaturally enhanced. We begin to see things we never thought we could comprehend in ways that we never could have imagined. We may not see fully now, but 1Cor 13:12 tells us that will change one day - *Now we see but a poor reflection as in a mirror; then we shall see face to face. Now*

I know in part; then I shall know fully, even as I am fully known. Until then, let's continue to keep our eyes on the Master. He certainly has His eye on us.

CHAPTER 12

THE WILD TOUR

Many years ago, I worked at a YMCA camp for an entire summer. One of my duties there was to take the senior high boys on an overnight expedition to a cave and underground lake called The Lost Sea. Like hundreds of other tourist stops across the country, The Lost Sea provided a commercial tour with lighted pathways and uniformed guides who hourly recited their canned narratives. It was interesting and nondescript at the same time and easily might have slipped into forgotten vacation stop oblivion, but for one thing. The Lost Sea offered something that distinguished them from the standard tourist stop. They had the *Wild Tour*.

Guided by local youths after the commercial tour closed for the day, the Wild Tour ventured beyond the ropes and footlights into the damp, muddy crannies illuminated only by our flashlights and lanterns. To a teenage boy (and a slightly older chaperone), this was adventure at its best. Following our guides, we hiked and climbed and crawled, occasionally pausing to investigate a bat or listen to a story of ancient Indian council fires. The experience lacked nothing and even included a series of rock passageways and tight squeezes our young guides made us negotiate to get from point to point.

One guide would approach a crevice and give instructions to follow him closely as he began to twist and contort through narrow passages that were not designed for the "larger boned" among us. One by one, my teens disappeared into the clefts; and I followed dutifully, praying each time that heavy machinery would not be required to extract me. The second guide would bring up the rear to make sure everyone made it safely through and then we would be led to another stack of rocks or a crack in the wall where we would start the process over again.

On my first trip to the cave, I accepted every challenge the guides presented to us. I knew some other "larger boned" counselors who had survived each test and I had purposed in my heart that if they could make it, I would too (the shame of heavy machinery would hold no candle to the shame of failure). On my second trip, I only participated in the challenges I enjoyed on trip one. On the third trip, I skipped even more of the process; but on the fourth trip, I decided to once again participate in the full experience. However, this time the guide who brought up the rear did something a little differently.

At the completion of one of the more difficult voyages through the rock, I took the help of an extended hand to get back on my feet. Imagine my surprise when I discovered the hand was attached to the guide I thought was behind me. He noticed my stunned expression and smiled mischievously, and I knew instantly we had been had. All of the crawling and squeezing was unnecessary---there was an alternate route the whole time. It was like crawling through the drawers and between the legs of your desk to get across it when all you had to do was walk around.

I said nothing; but when we got to the next little excursion, I pushed the last of my guys through the eye of the needle, turned to the guide and asked, "So, where is the walk-around?" He chuckled and motioned for me to follow him. We walked a few feet to the left, turned back to the right, and stepped around a boulder just in time to see my last spelunker exiting the rock with a look of triumph on his face. Naturally, I let him glory in his victory. I didn't have the heart to break it to him that we were all suckers!

Of course, there was no malice involved there. The guides didn't lead us through the narrow passages to be cruel. They knew after a while damp rocks and bats would become boring, so they added the alternate routes to provide adventure and tests for our skill and endurance. They had devised a plan to give us a memorable trip and it worked perfectly. I know I have never forgotten it. Still, looking back, I think about how we were truly at the mercy of our guides. We had no idea if there was one route, alternate routes, or if any route was safe, but the guides did. They knew how to get us in and get us out; and believe me---when you are hundreds of feet beneath solid rock, the getting out part becomes extremely important to you.

As Christians, getting through this world is extremely important to us. Many would tell you we are all heading to the same destination and that there are numerous routes to get there. Nothing could be further from the truth. We are not all heading to the same destination and there is definitely only one way to the destination to which most of us aspire. John 14:6 -- *Jesus answered, "I am the way and the truth and the life. No one comes to the Father except through me.*

Ironically, with the exception of the twists and turns, our path through Jesus is more like those tight passages in the cave than the easy walk-around. Matthew 7:13,14 explains it this way, *13 "Enter through the narrow gate. For wide is the gate and broad is the road that leads to destruction, and many enter through it. 14 But small is the gate and narrow the road that leads to life, and only a few find it.* Most people stumble around in the dark following a wide path, the path of least resistance, thinking they are heading toward their desired destination. Often they miss the narrow entrance that leads them out, that leads them to Salvation. Such were we before God shined the light of His Word on our path. Taking us by the hand, he negotiated the rocky paths for us and promised us that he would never leave us nor forsake us. Isaiah42:16 -- *I will lead the blind by ways they have not known, along unfamiliar paths I will guide them; I will turn the darkness into light before them and make the rough places smooth. These are the things I will do; I will not forsake them.*

Without reservation, we can step off the wide path so many are on and trust Jesus to guide us in the greatest adventure of life. Does this mean the "wild tour" we have embarked on will have no difficulties? Certainly not. It doesn't mean we know the way either. It does mean we are assured of the destination and we know *the* Way, a guide who will get us there safely. We can rest peacefully knowing the path He has chosen is the one that is best for us.

CHAPTER 13

TIME OUT AT THE TEA THYME CAFÉ

I can't help it. I have a meat and potatoes kind of body.
Actually, it's more like a pasta and too much dessert kind of
body; but why split hairs? If I wore tattoos, I would
probably have one of a donut right over my belly button.
You know, where the donut hole is centered right
ove....don't make me paint the picture; it wouldn't be pretty.
Suffice it to say that you wouldn't expect to see me at a
health food store, but that is exactly where I spend a lot of
time.

One of my favorite places to hang out is called The Herbal
Planet and Tea Thyme Café. I am on a first name basis with
all the staff; and I love to go there and enjoy a smoothie
while I write or surf the net. It is a nice relaxing atmosphere
and there are several Christians there, so I feel very
comfortable. Now I know that you don't really need a
detailed description of my relaxation habits, but I share this
small insight for a reason: you need to take a break. That's
right; you need to rest. I know that most of what I write is
designed to prod you, stimulate your thinking, or spur you

into action; but there comes a time when you need to get away for an hour, a day, or even a week.

Why do you need to take a break? Why are you so tired, though you probably haven't slowed down enough to even notice? Well, you might not realize it; but the population of this country is 273 million people. 140 million are retired. That leaves 133 million to do the work. There are 85 million in school, which leaves 48 million to do the work. Of this, there are 29 million employed by the federal government. This leaves 19 million to do the work. 2.8 million are in the armed forces preoccupied with protecting our country which leaves 16.2 million to do the work. Take from that total the 14,800,000 people who work for state and city governments, and that leaves 1.4 million to do the work. At any given time there are 188,000 people in hospitals, leaving 1,212,000 to do the work. Now, there are 1,211,998 people in prisons. That leaves just two people to do the work: you and me. No wonder we're so tired.

Alright, you probably aren't carrying half the nation's work load on your shoulders, but recharging our physical *and* spiritual batteries is still a necessity of life. Most of us understand the importance of physical rest. We are taught the importance of a good night's sleep as children, and God himself set the example of taking a periodic break from work by resting on the seventh day. However, do we understand the importance of spiritual rest? Jesus did. Matthew 11:28-30 - *28 "Come to me, all you who are weary and burdened, and I will give you rest. 29 Take my yoke upon you and learn from me, for I am gentle and humble in heart, and you will find rest for your souls. 30 For my yoke is easy and my burden is light."*

Jesus said in *Him* we would (not could) find rest for our souls. Isn't it interesting that we know with certainty the only place to find a spiritual rest, yet so often we search vainly elsewhere to find it? "....Oh, what peace we often forfeit. Oh, what needless pain we bear..." In turbulent times, as well as times of peace, it is always Jesus who is the one true haven. Psalm 62: 1, 2, 5-7 - *1 My soul finds rest in God alone; my salvation comes from him. 2 He alone is my rock and my salvation; he is my fortress, I will never be shaken. 5 Find rest, O my soul, in God alone; my hope comes from him. 6 He alone is my rock and my salvation; he is my fortress, I will not be shaken. 7 My salvation and my honor depend on God; he is my mighty rock, my refuge.*

I must be completely honest (as always). As much as I am convinced of what I am asserting here, there is no Scripture that I'm aware of that tells us directly, "You need spiritual rest". There are examples of Jesus withdrawing to be alone with just himself or a couple of His closest disciples, and there are examples of Jesus pulling all the disciples aside because they had not taken rest. Still, there is no specific teaching or instruction concerning spiritual rest. I wondered about this. An example is good enough for me, but I was still curious. If it really is important, wouldn't Jesus have addressed it directly?

As usual, I don't have all the answers; but I thought perhaps Jesus didn't address it directly because He knew we didn't need specific instruction in this area. You see, the mind and spirit are much stronger than the body. You can continue to push your body far beyond what it feels like it can do. That's how athletes train. If they stopped every time they felt like it, they would never develop or condition their bodies. Their minds and wills are stronger than their bodies, so they continue to push the physical beyond its perceived limitations to expand their overall ability and performance.

On the other hand, have you ever tried to think when your mind was ready to shut down? Or try to make your heart feel something it didn't want to feel? It doesn't work very well, does it? Our inner workings are much different than our outer workings. Our minds will shut down on us when they are overloaded; and to the point, our soul will seek out rest when it is overcome by turmoil. Maybe that is why Jesus spent His time talking about *where* to find rest rather than the need to take it.

Some people look for that peace and rest in the company of friends. Some search for it in sports, hobbies or even more work. Others think it can be found in introspection or seclusion, but there is a peace and rest that transcends all the earthly standards. It goes beyond what we could ever think or imagine and it can only be found one place: in Christ Jesus. John 14:27 - *Peace I leave with you; my peace I give you. I do not give to you as the world gives. Do not let your hearts be troubled and do not be afraid.*

Take a break and put up your feet. You probably deserve it. More importantly, take time to rest your spirit today. The how is not so important, but the who is critical. Spend time with Jesus. Get alone in your prayer closet or take a walk in the park. Bow your head at your desk or enjoy a cup of coffee at your favorite café; but some way, somehow, find that haven and fortress that can never be shaken. Psalm 62:1-4 -- *1 Hear my cry, O God; listen to my prayer. 2 From the ends of the earth I call to you, I call as my heart grows faint; lead me to the rock that is higher than I. 3 For you have been my refuge, a strong tower against the foe. 4 I long to dwell in your tent forever and take refuge in the shelter of your wings.*

CHAPTER 14

BAD COMPANY

Did your mother ever tell you, "Bad company corrupts good morals"? Mine didn't either, but she did pay close attention to who I spent time with; and I have a pretty good idea she understood the concept. Bad company isn't visitors who overstay their welcome and keep you up late at night. Bad company isn't a corporation that mishandles its assets, bilks its clients, or pollutes the environment. (Although, there is probably some bad company lurking around in there as well.) Bad Company isn't even a 70's rock and roll band (wait a minute....). Bad company can best be described as anyone who influences you in a manner contrary to the good moral standards found in Scripture.

"Hold on," you say. "That description could apply to half the people I know." Perhaps it does, but does that mean you have to isolate yourself or start warding off suspected bad influences with a crucifix? Probably not; but it does mean that in the real world, negative influences will prevail upon us daily and deliberately. We must recognize them and make sure that they do not prevail *over* us.

The challenge for the Christian is to be "in the world, but not of the world". We know we are supposed to be a light to the lost; but we're not sure if that means we're supposed to shine like a lighthouse on a remote hill, or light up the room when we walk through the door. Just how close are we supposed to be to those lost people? I'm not one to wear a WWJD bracelet, but we definitely need to ask the question here. What *would* Jesus do? The answer is clear. Jesus embraced the sinner (Mt 9:11, Lk 7:37-39, Lk 15:1, 2) ---- much to the chagrin of the religious leaders of the time. His actions were considered scandalous by those who were the experts in spiritual propriety.

"Okay, you are really confusing me," you say. "First you tell me to avoid bad company and then you tell me to embrace the sinner. What am *I* supposed to do???" Well, this is another example of the great balancing act in Scripture. We really need to do both, but how? Perhaps, if we look at the example of Jesus a little closer, we can get an idea how to reconcile the two. We know that Jesus was not afraid to rub elbows with sinners and that He had compassion on them, but where did His friendships lie? His closest friends were His disciples, men who shared His passion for the Father. It was in these relationships that He invested Himself.

From Jesus we learn that alliances are more important than associations, but we must never forget that associations can lead to alliances. Just as our associations with the world should be guided by compassion and purpose, Satan also endeavors to build associations with us with purpose. He understands the principle that associating leads to identifying which leads to bonding or allying. In other words, what initially feels like a feather can one day become a tether. If we are careless in our associations we can become entrapped in dangerous alliances. Consider Jehoshaphat.

Jehoshaphat was a godly ruler of the southern kingdom of Judah at a time when the northern kingdom of Israel was ruled by Ahab, an ungodly king. (You can read the story in its entirety in II Chronicles 18 and/or I Kings 22.) Initially, Jehoshaphat strengthened his position against Israel and Judah prospered; but for reasons not given in Scripture, Jehoshaphat later decided to ally himself by marriage with Ahab. Because of this alliance, when Ahab was about to go to war against Ramoth-gilead, he quickly enlisted Jehoshaphat's aid in battle. Jehoshaphat foolishly consented to make himself and all of his resources available to Ahab. Because of this decision, he almost lost his life. However, God mercifully intervened when Jehoshaphat called out to Him. II Chronicles 18:31,32 - *When the chariot commanders saw Jehoshaphat, they thought, "This is the king of Israel." So they turned to attack him, but Jehoshaphat cried out, and the Lord helped him. God drew them away from him, 32 for when the chariot commanders saw that he was not the king of Israel, they stopped pursuing him.*

This did not mean there were not consequences for Jehoshaphat's alliance. II Chronicles 19:1,2 - *When Jehoshaphat king of Judah returned safely to his palace in Jerusalem, 2 Jehu the seer, the son of Hanani, went out to meet him and said to the king, "Should you help the wicked and love those who hate the Lord? Because of this, the wrath of the Lord is upon you.* Jehoshaphat learned the hard way that bad alliances affect our relationship with God....or you would think he learned. II Chronicles 20:35-37 - *Later,*

Jehoshaphat king of Judah made an alliance with Ahaziah king of Israel, who was guilty of wickedness. 36 He agreed with him to construct a fleet of trading ships. After these were built at Ezion Geber, 37 Eliezer son of Dodavahu of Mareshah prophesied against Jehoshaphat, saying, "Because you have made an alliance with Ahaziah, the Lord will destroy what you have made." The ships were wrecked and were not able to set sail to trade.

Whether or not Jehoshaphat ever learned, the fact remains that bad company corrupts good morals....and produces bad results. God knows that we must associate with the world, but he will not share our affections. In fact, He says to be friends with the world is to be his enemy (James 4:4). Do not become enamored with the world, but rather let your passion for Christ lead you into alliances and friendships which will enhance your relationship with Him. Ecclesiastes 4:12 - *Though one may be overpowered, two can defend themselves. A cord of three strands is not quickly broken.* As members of the Body of Christ we can cultivate wonderful relationships because we are in the best possible company. Your mother will be proud; and more importantly, Jesus will be too.

CHAPTER 15

ITTY BITTY, TEENIE WEENIE FAITH

Once, two nuns were returning to the convent after a long day of service at the local hospital. About half-way home their car ran out of gas. The poor sisters did not have a gas can with them, and could find nothing in their car with which to fetch fuel except a hospital bed pan. Slightly embarrassed, they realized using the bed pan was the only way to get gas into the tank; and soon they had trekked to a nearby station and returned with the needed fuel. As the nuns were pouring the gas into the tank, two priests who were enjoying a rousing theological debate drove by in their own car. Observing the scene, one priest turned to the other and said, "Now, *that's* faith!"

Faith is one of those things that is difficult to measure. Many of us have been able to quote Hebrews 11:1 since we were children and know that "faith is the substance of things hoped for, the evidence of things not seen"; but what does that mean? For most of us it means we can't see faith; it is an intangible entity. In the sense that it is not visible and does not have a physical body, perhaps it could be described as intangible; but in the sense that it is actual and effectual in nature, it is extremely tangible. Moreover, our difficulty in measuring faith doesn't mean that it cannot be measured. Jesus measured it on a regular basis.

The gospels are full of instances where Jesus answered someone's request by making an assessment of their faith. Isn't it interesting that when Jesus did make commentary on someone's faith it was always on one end of the spectrum or the other? He rarely, if ever, talked about the middle ground. We never hear "Oh you of average faith" or "Oh woman, ordinary is your faith". No, Jesus has always been able to read faith like we read a thermometer; and His keen eye is quick to spot our highs and lows. Perhaps we would pray like the disciples: "Lord, increase our faith". It certainly is a noble request. However, Jesus' answer to their request dealt with what you could do with just a small amount of faith. I want to look at that and a person who, according to Jesus, had "little faith". Luke 17:5, 6 - *5 The apostles said to the Lord, "Increase our faith!" 6 He replied, "If you have faith as small as a mustard seed, you can say to this mulberry tree, 'Be uprooted and planted in the sea,' and it will obey you.*

Our first observation is the size of the faith we need for this miracle. Everyone knows seeds are small; but if you have never planted a garden or had a Sunday school teacher bring seeds into class for an illustration, then you might not know how small mustard seeds actually are. Since I can't place one in your hand, just take a look at the period at the end of this sentence and you'll get a pretty good idea what one looks like. .. Hey, there's a couple more. The actual seeds are slightly larger, but only slightly. You see the point Jesus

77

was making: it doesn't take a lot of faith.

Our second observation is the size of the miracle. Trees of this type could reach 70 to 80 feet in height and were not objects that could be moved easily. Cutting the tree down and hauling it off would have been a bit of a job in itself, but causing it to be uprooted would be impossible for a single human being. Besides, who would think of doing such a thing? Consider how audacious it was to propose that one could uproot the tree, let alone transport it to the sea to be replanted. And this was to be done by word of mouth only? What was Jesus saying? He was saying we can't begin to imagine the proportion of the miracles He can perform through us.

Our final observation is the deeper meaning of Jesus' illustration. Was Jesus simply saying that a little faith can produce a giant miracle or was there more to His example? Begin by looking at what prompted the disciples' request to have their faith increased. Jesus had just instructed them on the dangers of sin and offense. He had told them to forgive their brother every time he repented, even if he offended them repeatedly. This seemed like a hard thing to them. Bitterness can be a powerful fixation. And why did Jesus use a mulberry tree? Was there one growing right there making a perfect illustration? Perhaps, but let's look a little closer at that tree.

With a little research we find that there are several types of mulberry trees. One that was prominent in this region was the white mulberry. Today the white mulberry is sometimes considered a weed tree, something that is a nuisance and needs to be removed. Hmmm. That would be interesting if

Jesus was referring to that specific tree, but upon further investigation we discover the tree Jesus spoke of was probably not a mulberry at all. The Greek word here indicates a mulberry *like* tree called a sycamine. The sycamine and the mulberry were similar in appearance. In fact, even their fruit was almost identical -- with one huge difference: while the fruit of the mulberry tree was sweet and delicious, the sycamine fruit was extremely bitter. Now, that is interesting.

Finally, did you notice that Jesus did not say the tree would be *cast* into the sea? He said it would be planted there. Where are things planted? In the soil. Where is soil in the sea? On the sea floor. Jesus wasn't satisfied to have the tree covered with a little water, He wanted it buried and anchored at the bottom of the sea. It speaks of permanence and finality. Why is this important? I respectfully submit that Jesus wasn't telling his disciples (or us) that huge parlor tricks can be performed with a little bit of faith. He was explaining how our seed of faith in Him can overcome the mightiest problems we will face, even the root of bitterness. Through faith we can have ultimate victory. It has been said that since we all possess a measure of faith, it is not the quantity of our faith that matters; it is the quality. I believe that to be true. Faith is like skunk scent -- the real thing goes a long way. (Father, forgive me for that analogy.)

Who was the person with little faith? Well, Jesus described several people that way; but what may surprise us is the fact that he addressed one of his own disciples in this manner. Matthew 14:25-31 - *25 During the fourth watch of the night Jesus went out to them, walking on the lake. 26 When the disciples saw him walking on the lake, they were terrified.*

"It's a ghost," they said, and cried out in fear. 27 But Jesus immediately said to them: "Take courage! It is I. Don't be afraid." 28 "Lord, if it's you," Peter replied, "tell me to come to you on the water." 29 "Come," he said. Then Peter got down out of the boat, walked on the water and came toward Jesus. 30 But when he saw the wind, he was afraid and, beginning to sink, cried out, "Lord, save me!" 31 Immediately Jesus reached out his hand and caught him. "You of little faith," he said, "why did you doubt?"

Peter often gets a bad rap here for not having faith, but how many people do you know who have walked on water? Peter can claim membership in a pretty exclusive club when it comes to water walkers. Considering Peter actually jumped out of the boat and walked on water toward Jesus, I'm guessing his "little faith" wasn't the problem. I'm thinking the problem came when he let doubt creep in, when he stopped looking at Jesus and started looking at circumstances. Don't worry about the quantity of your faith; you have enough. Just start exercising what you have. Who knows what you can accomplish through Christ? Wouldn't it be exciting to find out?

CHAPTER 16

SAVE THE HONEY BUNS!

I have a good friend who has a bread route and a brother who has a snack vending business. They deal with slightly different food products, but they both have a common enemy---stales. Stales are the products which have been on the shelf or in a vending machine too long and have lost their freshness. They can no longer be sold and have lost their worth to the vendors. These stales are, at best, a time consuming inconvenience and, at worst, a loss of profit. In my friend's case, he is able to move the product at a discount store that handles the older merchandise. In my brother's case, he is forced to eat the loss. (Oh yeah---pun definitely intended!)

I have worked with my brother on his route, and I will never forget the first time he handed me a half dozen honey buns and said, "Throw these in that trash can over there." What horror of horrors was this?!? Throw honey buns *away*? I dragged my feet on the way to the waste basket and with one last, tender caress let the beautiful pastries fall from my fingers into the can. I thought about how much I like honey buns, about starving children in third world countries, about how much I like honey buns, and I wondered what kind of organization I could form to help save the cast away pastries. However, when my brother had me sample one of the stale buns, I canceled my call to the UN. It was horrible. It wasn't the soft, tasty treat I craved; it was hard, chewy, and bland.

Thinking about these wasted food items reminded me of two similar examples in the Bible---one in the Old Testament and one in the New. The first is found in Exodus 16 and is the story of God's provision for the children of Israel in the form of manna. Manna is a mystical substance to us because we have never seen it. All we know about manna is it was like flakes in texture, white in appearance like coriander seed, and like honey in taste.(v.14,31) There were also instructions for gathering manna and consequences for disobedience found in verses 16-20 - *16 This is what the Lord has commanded: 'Each one is to gather as much as he needs. Take an omer for each person you have in your tent.'" 17 The Israelites did as they were told; some gathered much, some little. 18 And when they measured it by the omer, he who gathered much did not have too much, and he who gathered little did not have too little. Each one gathered as much as he needed. 19 Then Moses said to them, "No one is to keep any of it until morning." 20 However, some of them paid no attention to Moses; they kept part of it until morning, but it was full of maggots and began to smell. So Moses was angry with them.*

How interesting. The manna had an expiration date! If the Israelites kept it longer than instructed, it went bad---and in a hurry. The manna was designed for use, not storage. There was always enough, more than enough, but any attempt to hoard the provision produced a stinky result. I don't know if this is where the adage, "Use it or lose it" found its origin, but it certainly applies. What do we have that is designed for use, not storage? Talents? Resources? You might not smell the stinky result if you don't use what has been entrusted to you, but I'm guessing someone else out there might.

The second example is found in Mt 5:13 - *"You are the salt of the earth. But if the salt loses its saltiness, how can it be made salty again? It is no longer good for anything, except to be thrown out and trampled by men."*
Salt is important today, but it is relatively cheap. You can buy a box of salt for pocket change; but in ancient times, it was an extremely valuable commodity. In fact, the term "to be worth one's salt" originates from an early practice in which Roman soldiers were paid their wages in salt. If a man didn't earn his wage, he wasn't "worth his salt". The problem with salt as legal tender is that there is the potential for it to lose its savor; and without its savor, salt becomes useless. Can you imagine your paycheck losing its effectiveness? Well..., perhaps that is a bad example. The point is it doesn't matter what value is attached to any given thing. If that thing can no longer serve its given purpose, it becomes useless.

Trying to make an application after that statement seems reduntantly redundant. Our specific purposes may vary, but our general purpose is the same --- service to God. Everything else centers on the fact that we were designed for His good pleasure. We have the option to be used or be refused, but no other choices seem to be available. If salt loses its saltiness, what is it good for?

My brother has been selling snacks for years and, through his experience, has learned what stales can be salvaged and what should be thrown away. Many times, I have seen him give the product a little squeeze to check its softness or to see if the package was properly sealed. Some are fine for a period after their expiration date; and though they can no longer be sold, he salvages them for personal use or to give to friends and family. (Many of which I have been a happy recipient, I might add.) On the other hand, some of the product is disposed of because it is beyond any use whatsoever.

We, too, have an expiration date; and when that date arrives, a determination will be made about us. Will we be found fresh and retainable or will we be cast away? Some might think this a harsh concept. "God is a God of love. He would never throw us away." Yes, He will, my friend. As much as it will break His heart, He will cast away into eternal darkness those who are not fresh and useful, those who are not salty. Jesus speaks of it three separate times in the book of Matthew---Mt 8:12, Mt 22:13, and Mt 25:30 which reads - 30 And throw that worthless servant outside, into the darkness, where there will be weeping and gnashing of teeth.'

Granted, it is a sobering thought to think that one day we will be judged regarding our value to the kingdom. I have often heard ministers make a statement similar to this: "One day we will stand before Almighty God and be required to answer the question, 'What did you do with my Son, Jesus?'". The statement usually focuses on whether or not we have accepted Jesus Christ as Savior. As Christians, I believe that the question should go a little deeper. In light of an expectation on our lives, what are we doing *with God's* Son, Jesus? Are we working with Him? Is He working through us? Remember we will expire one day if the Lord doesn't return first. Either way, maybe it would be a good idea to give *ourselves* a little "squeeze test" from time to time. We want to be found fresh and usable when the Master calls.

CHAPTER 17

LORD, GIVE ME PATIENCE
(AND GIVE IT TO ME NOW)

There was once a man from the city who was visiting a small farm; and during this visit, he saw a farmer feeding pigs in a most extraordinary manner. The farmer would lift a pig up to a nearby apple tree, and the pig would eat the apples off the tree directly. The farmer would move the pig from one apple to another until the pig was satisfied; then he would start again with another pig. The city man watched this activity for some time with great astonishment. Finally, he could not resist saying to the farmer, "This is the most inefficient method of feeding pigs that I can imagine. Just think of the time that would be saved if you simply shook the apples off the tree and let the pigs eat them from the ground!" The farmer looked puzzled and replied, "What's time to a pig?"

Some of us are blessed with an ample supply of patience and others of us are not. I are not. I wish I had more patience. I've prayed patiently and patiently waited for a patient patience, but it somehow seems to elude me. Perhaps you've prayed for patience like I have. *Dear Lord, please give me patience....I'll wait right here for it Lord....Right here, Lord, I'm waiting right here...Still here, Lord....Right here....Yep, that's me, Lord....waiting right here....Lord?.....LORD?....Why won't you give me patience, Lord?* There are a lot of variations, but you get the drift. Unfortunately, I don't know anyone who has taken that approach and received an endowment of patience. However, be careful what you pray for. God may not drop patience on you with a little red bow, but that doesn't mean He won't answer your prayer. More on that later.

One of the greatest determining factors of patience is perspective. By this I mean that the fast paced, drive through, microwave, "give it to me now" society we live in can skewer our thought processes in such a way that we might come to believe that waiting a whole 7 minutes for our happy meal at McDonalds is exhibiting "real" patience. Where would our patience levels be if we didn't live in such a high speed world and if our society didn't always push for "faster and faster"? I have to believe that the most impatient persons of a century ago would appear pretty patient today. Most likely even our contemporaries in slower paced cultures or less technologically advanced areas have a different view of patience. Having a God view on life where we believe He has everything under control and works all together for our good also makes patience a more durable entity. It all comes down to perspective. As Christians we need a biblical perspective, so let's look at examples of patience in Scripture.

The first example is a great one for young people who are anxious to get married. It's the story of Jacob and Rachel, or maybe I should say Jacob and *Leah* and Rachel. The story is found in Genesis 29 and tells how Jacob fell in love with Rachel and struck a deal with her father to work seven years for her hand in marriage. Seven years? Today you're lucky if an engagement lasts seven months. However, Jacob was diligent and patient; and at the end of seven years, he was ready to marry his bride. Unfortunately for Jacob, there was a little twist involved. Laban, Rachel's father, pulled a fast one on Jacob on the wedding day and walked his oldest daughter, Leah, down the aisle instead of Rachel. Poor Jacob didn't catch on until the knot had been tied. He eventually married Rachel as well, but he had to obligate himself to another seven years of labor. Fourteen years of labor for one woman. You can call it true love or insanity, but either way you have to call it patience.

Jacob exhibited the waiting aspect of patience; Job showed us its enduring side. We have all heard the phrase "the patience of Job"; but not many of us have aspired to that kind of virtue------especially if we have to go through what he went through to get it. His story is so compelling that there is an entire book devoted to it and one of the most compelling elements of that story is the fact that Job did nothing to deserve the terrible affliction that came upon him. That's what makes his patience so amazing. If we endure punishment when we deserve it, what great virtue have we shown? It's enduring punishment for righteousness' sake that is commendable. 1 Peter 2:20 - *But how is it to your credit if you receive a beating for doing wrong and endure it? But if you suffer for doing good and you endure it, this is commendable before God.*

Sometimes patience is waiting and sometimes it is enduring.

Sometimes it is both. Joseph had the good fortune to receive the double whammy. Not only was he falsely imprisoned, he also had to wait several years before the promises God gave him came to fruition. Given a dream of his own future at 17 years old, Joseph would be well into his adulthood before he would be summoned to interpret Pharaoh's dream and be elevated to leadership. He was abused by family members and imprisoned by foreigners, yet we never read where Joseph wavered in his faith or doubted God's promise. Patience is a close cousin to faith. Trust in God allows us to wait and endure when others are overcome with anxiety.

I told you we would get back to God answering your prayer for patience, and now I am about to share with you one of the most confounding portions of Scripture I know. James 1:2-4 -- *2 Consider it pure joy, my brothers, whenever you face trials of many kinds, 3 because you know that the testing of your faith develops perseverance (patience). 4 Perseverance (Patience) must finish its work so that you may be mature and complete, not lacking anything.* Great! To get patience, we have to endure more trials and temptations; and on top of that, I have to be happy about it? That's why I was praying for patience in the first place. If I was mature, complete, and not lacking anything, I wouldn't need patience.

Okay, maybe I'm overreacting. Perhaps, like you, I see that patience is a virtue worthy to be sought after; and like anything of great value, its extraordinary worth merits extraordinary effort to attain it. Recognizing the end reward enables us to "consider it pure joy" when we have to face trials to get there. I never minded waiting on my mother when she was working in the kitchen because I knew the end result was going to be great. How much more should I be willing to wait on my Heavenly Father? He always has something great planned for me.

CHAPTER 18

LEFTOVERS

I love leftovers. I love food in general, but leftovers are great. The only thing better than enjoying a wonderful home cooked meal is knowing you can enjoy it again later without all the toil and preparation. And of course, some things are better the second time around. Chili comes to mind, and then there's turkey. As a child (and adult), I loved my mother's incredible Thanksgiving feasts; but as much as I enjoyed the wonderful meal, I would be dreaming of those turkey sandwiches we would have later that evening even as I stuffed my face with dressing (or dressed my face with stuffing, depending on what part of the country you're from).

My mother, like many great cooks, had the ability to take leftovers and turn them into some delectable dish. Nothing went to waste at our house. Leftover cream of wheat would be cut into strips, lightly pan fried, and sprinkled with cinnamon and sugar to make a sweet snack. Leftover vegetables from today's meal would find their way into tomorrow's casserole. "Waste not, want not" was always in practice in Mama's kitchen. However, my mother's creative culinary skills were not confined to leftovers. She could whip up something out of nothing it seemed. "Okay what do we have in the pantry?.....Tomato paste, condensed milk, a jar of pickles, and a can of corn? That will be enough. Bring it here." (Of course you have to imagine that spoken with an Italian accent to get the full effect). Reluctantly, I would bring the ingredients to her, certain in my heart that this time my dear mama had overreached her considerable skill. She never disappointed though. Somehow, no matter how strange a list of ingredients she started with, my mother would put something great to eat on the table. And believe me---if my mama put something on the table, you wanted to eat it! (By the way, the above list of ingredients was an example. I do not remember my mother ever using that exact combination. PLEASE, do not try that recipe at home!)

With all the turkey and food references, you probably thought the Thanksgiving holiday prompted these thoughts; but it didn't. I actually began to think about these things when I heard a television evangelist prompt his listeners to make a donation by saying, "God will use what you have". I thought this was a viable truth, however he said this immediately after his associate had relayed that 3000 of us needed to send in 100 bucks apiece. I'm no genius, but I was pretty sure that those 3000 and the thousands of other listeners all came from various economic standings. I was equally sure that 100 dollars to one might have been nothing, whereas it might have been all the grocery money of another. *And* I was *POSITIVE* that Joseph didn't have 100 dollars to send. This brought me back to the viable truth---God will use what you have.

Don't worry, this writing is not going to culminate with a

donation request because I don't have any tapes or jewelry to send out thanking you for your generous contribution; but I do want to look at the principle of making what we have available to God. The Bible is full of examples of God using whatever was available to accomplish miraculous works, either directly or through His servants. It began in the Garden of Eden when God himself made garments of animal skin to clothe Adam and Eve. If that is not miraculous enough for you, consider Moses appearing before Pharaoh. God used the simple staff that Moses carried to perform miracles before Pharaoh and later before the children of Israel. Elijah told the widow to bring him what she had and she never ran out of food, Elisha cut a stick and threw it in the water to make an axe head float, and Jesus spit in the dirt to make mud for healing a blind man's eyes. The list goes on, but my favorite story is about the little boy who gave his lunch to Jesus so He could feed 5000 people.

You remember the story. A large group of people had traveled to the mountainside to hear Jesus teach and now, away from the market and any source of food, they were hungry. Jesus had compassion on the crowd but also saw an excellent opportunity to teach his disciples; and testing their faith, He instructed them to feed the crowd. Obviously, the disciples were daunted by the task. John 6:9 - *Philip answered him, "Eight months' wages would not buy enough bread for each one to have a bite!"* Jesus knew that the situation looked tough, but He also knew any investment of faith was going to produce a miracle that day. Enter a little boy.

John 6:8,9 - *8 Another of his disciples, Andrew, Simon Peter's brother, spoke up, 9 "Here is a boy with five small barley loaves and two small fish, but how far will they go among so many?"* Have you ever thought about what was going through the boy's mind when he offered up his lunch? Was he mad because the disciple's snatched it from him and confiscated it? Did he offer it out of good manners thinking no one would really take him up on the offer? Or did he offer it willingly and cheerfully, wanting to do whatever he could to help? I want to believe the latter; but whatever his motivation for giving was, I'm pretty sure he had no clue what the outcome would be. Still, this boy and the disciples found out that God specializes in creating things out of nothing. They shouldn't have been surprised and neither should we. Look at the universe for goodness sake. He's been at this for years.

Just like that skilled cook can take whatever is on hand, no matter how odd the ingredients, and create something good to eat; God loves to take our meager offerings, no matter how insignificant they may seem, and create miracles. The boy might have thought that his little offering would only be part of a much larger plan. On another day, he might have been right. Jesus might have used a different miracle. But on this day, on the side of a mountain near the Sea of Galilee, his offering *was* the plan. This boy had no way of knowing and neither do we. We don't know what God will do with our offering; but just like the boy, we have to make it and ourselves available. Whether it is our lunch or our last penny like the widow's mite, we need only offer it up willingly and cheerfully. God will do the rest.

There is one last thing. I said that I love leftovers; God, however, does not. He is seeking our first fruits. This may not seem like a big deal, but read the story of Cain and Able in Genesis 4 and you will see that bringing "some" and bringing the "first fruit" are vastly different in God's economy. The little boy did not offer fish bones and a gnawed roll. He offered his best and because he did there were 12 baskets of leftovers. Now that's the kind of leftovers I'm talking about!

CHAPTER 19

SPIRITUAL INERTIA

I was driving down a country highway when a gallon jug was blown from the open bed of the truck I was following. This appeared to be the standard container that would hold oil or antifreeze, and something you would commonly find on a work truck. I had seen things blown out of vehicles before, so this wasn't extremely unusual. However, my attention was captured by what happened next. The jug fell to the highway, but continued to speed down the road almost as if it were trying to catch the truck it had just fallen from. I am certainly not a science major, but I immediately recognized the properties of inertia. The jug was light enough to be blown out of the truck, but it still contained enough fluid (mass) to keep it moving rapidly down the highway---for a short period of time.

I followed the jug for 2-3 seconds before catching up to it and blowing past. The jug had lost the effect of the power (the truck) being applied to it and a new power (friction) had taken over. My twisted mind quickly began to process the information it had just received. If my vehicle were to come to a sudden and complete stop, I would continue through the windshield and down the highway just like the jug. How much friction would be applied to my ample backside before *I* came to a complete stop? I was significantly heavier than said jug, so I could only assume I would travel quite a distance farther. Of course, there would be a lot more friction on said backside. I forgot about the speed and distances and promptly decided this would not be a way I would want to make my backside less ample.

Sir Isaac Newton defined inertia in Definition 3 of his <u>Philosophi Naturalis Principia Mathmatica</u> which states: (1) *The vis insita, or innate force of matter is a power of resisting, by which every body, as much as in it lies, endeavors to preserve in its present state, whether it be of rest, or of moving uniformly forward in a right line.* We understand this as Newton's First Law of Motion which in simple terms means, "A body in motion tends to remain in motion; a body at rest tends to remain at rest." So just like the jug, when an object gets moving it wants to keep moving; and it will keep going and going (think Energizer Bunny) until a force (gravity, friction) acts upon it. Conversely, if an object is just sitting there, it's going to keep sitting there until it experiences some kind of force.

Isn't it interesting that we have a "spiritual inertia" that acts in much the same way? Have you ever noticed the more active we become for Christ in sharing our faith or in some type of ministry, the more easily we can remain active. What once seemed difficult or audacious now seems simple or normal. Our activity gives us momentum or "spiritual inertia". Likewise, the longer we sit on our ample spiritual backsides, the harder it is to get going and become spiritually active. Unfortunately, when we find a comfortable place on that padded pew, we "tend to remain at rest".

We also have spiritual forces at work in our lives. Friction isn't just a scientific term. It is also a powerful force in the spiritual realm that Satan has used to slow the momentum of more than one Christian. Gravity is another force that can affect us spiritually. Complacency can have a gravitational pull that keeps us at rest; or if we do launch out on a lofty endeavor, we may feel like those around us are trying to "bring us down".

Thankfully, there is a force acting on our behalf that is more powerful than any force of evil. That force is in the person of the Holy Spirit and the power He brings. Jesus gave the promise of this power in Acts 1:8 -- *"But you will receive power when the Holy Spirit comes on you; and you will be my witnesses in Jerusalem, and in all Judea and Samaria, and to the ends of the earth."* What an amazing thought that we have the very Person of God residing within us to be our empowerment. Now there is an irresistible force!

Peter experienced this power along with about 120 other believers in the Upper Room on the Day of Pentecost. It was then that he learned the difference between brashness and boldness, between enthusiasm and power. Peter was never one to have a problem talking the talk, but like many of us, he sometimes had problems walking the walk. His enthusiasm was never called into question. After all, Peter was the one who swore he would never leave Jesus, the one who cut off the ear of the Roman soldier, the one who stepped out of the boat and walked on water toward the Master. Yet, in all those instances Peter was in over his head (particularly when the walking on water thing didn't pan out). He did not have the power to sustain his rhetoric or even his actions. Jesus had always bailed him out, but what would happen now that He had ascended?

Fortunately, just as He still does today, God had everything under control. With the ascension of Christ came the advent of the Holy Spirit...and the power we need. You can almost see a visible change in Peter as he stood to address the gathering crowd. As he answered their skepticism and preached the good news, he experienced a power he had never imagined. No longer did God reside *with* him; now God resided *in* him. And the results were phenomenal. We have no other records of Peter's sermons; but I'm guessing he never had 300 converts at one time, let alone 3000. I know that the genuine article cannot be judged by results alone, but I also know that the genuine article will always bear results. And, as Peter found out, the Holy Spirit is the genuine article.

If you feel overwhelmed by the forces of this world, be encouraged. God's power is greater. If you feel drained like a used up battery, be of good cheer. The Holy Spirit can energize you. If you feel like you do not have the strength to complete this journey and the tasks at hand, do not give up. His grace and power are sufficient for you. He will be your strength. He will be your power. He will be the spiritual inertia that keeps you going.

CHAPTER 20

DO OVERS

Anyone who has played any kind of childhood game knows what do overs are. Remember when it was your turn to kick in kickball and you gathered all the energy your little body could muster for that one kick that would burst the ball into tiny pieces? You stood there poised to annihilate the ball; and then kicking wildly, you missed it altogether. What did you do then? You called do overs, of course! You were somehow distracted or you slipped or the ball took a bad hop---it didn't matter what the excuse was; you had invoked the sacred right of do overs and nobody would deny you your second chance. Why? Because everyone else knew they would need a do over for themselves sometime.

Somewhere around 2nd or 3rd grade the competitive edge took over and do overs become disallowed. We no longer requested them for fear of being labeled a baby; but deep inside, whenever we messed up, we wanted our do overs. Actually, we still do.

Today, most popular games are computer based and can be manipulated to produce about as many do overs as you please. I have to confess that I have certain affection (ahem…addiction…ahem) for one myself. It is the game of spider solitaire. It is on my computer, and I have to be extremely careful not to become absorbed in what I intend to be a "quick" game. My momentary diversion or "mental exercise", as I like to call it, often becomes an hour of mental anguish as I refuse to give in to a piece of machinery. The problem with spider solitaire is there are many options, but only a few allow you to clear the board.

Fortunately, the computer version of the game is equipped with an *undo* button which allows me to attempt various combinations until I discover the one that works. Obviously, this is not cheating. Since the button was provided, it is clear to me that someone intended it to be used. Consequently, the only way I can be defeated at spider solitaire is to succumb to time constraints---something, I must confess, I don't do nearly enough. So, in the interest of time stewardship, I have chosen to play less and less solitaire. The point I am making is not that I use the button or that we all desire to have do overs on occasion. The point is that games often have them and life seldom does.

There are few times, if any, in life when we get a free pass--- a real do over. Sure, there are many times in life when we escape punishment, but how many times do we escape consequence? The deed you hoped no one would find out about may have escaped detection, but there is more to it than that, isn't there? The deed is done and cannot be erased. You and God know what happened even if no one else does, and your conscience bears the weight of the deed. Perhaps, though no blame is assigned, you can still see the deed's effects in other people's lives; and if not theirs, then certainly you can see that your own character has been altered. Naturally, these actions could be anything from the sinister to the benign. Our example might be some hidden sin, but it could just as easily be a carelessly spoken word. The fact is, whether righteous or evil, our words and deeds are just like the toothpaste squeezed out of the tube; once they go out, they don't go back in.

They do, however, *come* back in. We can't retrieve our words and deeds, but we do reap a harvest from them. Good words and deeds reap a good harvest and bad words and deeds reap a bad harvest. Since we are stuck with a system of cause and effect, reward and consequence, and we have no do overs, it is imperative that we pay close attention to our words and deeds. The scripture makes clear the importance of the choices we make. Galatians 6:7, 8 says, *"7 Do not be deceived: God cannot be mocked. A man reaps what he sows. 8 The one who sows to please his sinful nature, from that nature will reap destruction; the one who sows to please the Spirit, from the Spirit will reap eternal life."*

The good news is we have a choice about the words and deeds we sow. We can choose life over death. That is incredible. God, the ultimate author of liberty, allows us the choice of our eternal destination. The decision is made in what we do with His Son, Jesus, and the subsequent daily choices that we make. Daily choices? Am I trying to say that there is more to salvation than a profession of faith? Well…in a word, yes. I am not saying we are saved by works. As Paul would say, "God forbid". I am saying what James *and* Paul said. Our faith is demonstrated by our works and our fruit is indicative of our roots.

James 2:17-- *"In the same way, faith by itself, if it is not accompanied by action, is dead."*

Titus 3:8-- *"This is a faithful saying, and these things I want you to affirm constantly, that those who have believed in God should be careful to maintain good works. These things are good and profitable to men."*

Titus 3:14-- *"And let our people also learn to maintain good works, to meet urgent needs, that they may not be unfruitful."*

Deeds. Choices. Works. Call them what you will, but the fact is the kind of faith we possess will produce a tangible fruit. I don't think I can stress this point more; but in emphasizing the importance of our choices, I may have been a little deceptive. I shared the good news, but there is even better news. The *great* news is we can still have do overs...of a sort. While it is true that the consequences of our words and deeds cannot be naturally erased, God promises us a clean slate spiritually when we come to him and confess our transgressions. 1 John 1:9 -- *If we confess our sins, he is faithful and just and will forgive us our sins and purify us from all unrighteousness.*

Although God usually chooses not to intervene in natural consequence, He longs to come to our aid in the more important area of spiritual consequence. In fact, He specializes in it. Maybe God knows that we need physical consequence to better make the choices affecting spiritual consequence. I don't know why His design works this way. Thankfully, His ways are much higher than mine. I only know that He has a master plan and it mercifully includes spiritual do overs. It's called grace.

CHAPTER 21

WE'RE OFF TO SEE THE WIZARD

I don't know how I missed it. I never realized it; but Frank Baum's classic children's story, *The Wonderful Wizard of Oz*, might very easily have been a parable about Christians. There are streets of gold, jeweled cities, and there's that Dorothy girl who is lost and is trying to find her way home. Best of all, there are three types of Christians represented by the characters that Dorothy encounters. Think about it. Have you met Scarecrow Christians (no brains)? Tin Man Christians (no heart)? Cowardly Lion Christians (no courage)? Let's explore that.

Scarecrow Christians

One of my favorite Mark Rutland quotes is, "As Christians, we are not required to check our brains at the door when we walk into a church service." He was referring to the tendency some have to suspend critical thinking in the name of "being led by the Spirit". Being led by the Spirit is integral to any true worship experience, sermon delivery, or teaching session; but so is critical thinking. If you aren't using the mind that God gave you then how are you going to know you are indeed being led by the Spirit? Are you going to depend on your "feelings"? Good luck. I just hope that you "feel" okay when you enter the service so your discernment is on track.

Of course that is silly. We don't discern by feeling. We certainly want to be sensitive to the direction of the Holy Spirit, but we also use our brains in measuring what we see, hear, and feel against the standard of Scripture that God has given us. For instance, if you *feel* the Spirit is leading you to do something that is contrary to Scripture, then your *mind* should tell you the feeling is the pepperoni pizza you ate last night and not the Holy Spirit. Furthermore, we know we are able to judge people and situations by the fruit they produce. Do we judge fruit with our spirit? By our feelings? No, we judge fruit with a discerning mind. Utilize the brain you have been given. It honors Him just as your sensitivity to His Spirit does.

Tin Man Christians

Christians with no heart are those who call themselves by the name of Christ and yet understand nothing of His love or compassion. Love, kindness, and mercy are the very essence of Jesus. They were what brought Him to earth the first time and what will allow us to go to Him when He returns. To truly understand His love will cause two other wonderful byproducts to manifest themselves in your life---peace and joy. Few things are sadder than to see someone who claims to be a Christian walking around sad, sour, or worse....synical. (I know cynical starts with a "c", but I have the "s" thing working here.)

There is a story about Alexander the Great having a young deserter brought before him to be questioned. "What's your name?" Alexander asked. "Alexander", replied the terrified lad. "Alexander?" bellowed the conqueror. "Boy, either change your ways or change your name." Apparently, Alexander was not willing to be embarrassed by a coward wearing the same name as he. Do you think it's possible that we embarrass Christ in much the same way when we walk through life wearing His name yet never showing a shred of compassion to those around us? Freely you have received; freely give.

Cowardly Lion Christians

Cowardly Christians should be an oxymoron, but sadly we find that Christians with courage are often hard to find. We have brash Christians and arrogant Christians, but truly courageous ones? Now, that's another story. We appear to be afraid of most anything. We're afraid of witnessing, of what our peers might think, of leading, of following, of being politically incorrect, and of Satan himself. In *The Wizard of Oz* the cowardly lion felt as if he were born to be a coward.
Yeah, it's sad, believe me Missy
When you're born to be a sissy
Without the vim and verve.
But I could show my prowess
Be a lion, not a mowess
If I only had the nerve.
Fortunately, he discovered that he wasn't born into cowardice; and neither are we---at least not when we are born again. As Christians, our boldness and courage should be something that makes others sit up and take notice. Acts

107

4:13 - *When they saw the courage of Peter and John and realized that they were unschooled, ordinary men, they were astonished and they took note that these men had been with Jesus.* When we encounter Jesus and are full of His Holy Spirit (Acts 4:8), we are able to step out into areas we never thought possible.

In fact, the Holy Spirit chases all of those Oz characters away. 2Timothy 1:7 - *For God has not given us a spirit of fear, but of power* (no more cowardly lion) *and of love* (no more tin man) *and of a sound mind* (no more scarecrow). If you have found any or all of these characters creeping up in your own spiritual walk, do not despair. God is greater than any wizard and He is no charlatan. He can renew your mind, repair your heart, and restore your courage. And the best part is you don't have to go on some great journey. All you have to do is call on His name. At the end of the movie, *The Wizard of Oz*, Dorothy discovered that she had the ability to go home the whole time. Isn't it great to know that we can too?

CHAPTER 22

YES, LORD, I WILL RIDE

Perhaps you are familiar with the worship song, "Yes, Lord, We Will Ride With You". It is an extremely moving song; and if it happens to be your favorite worship song, then by all means, you keep singing it. I just have a little bit of a problem with it -- it doesn't seem to be very accurate to me. I know. Far be it from me, the one whose mind works like a side to side elevator, to be critical of anyone's artistic license. But, believe it or not, I can still be pretty fanatical about little things like accuracy.

My whole problem lies in the repeated line that Jesus is riding on a white horse all across this land. Jesus will *return* on a white horse, but I find nothing that tells me He is canvassing the countryside on one right now. And why is it just *this* land. That seems pretty arrogant to me. Wouldn't Jesus want people from all over the world to ride with Him? They certainly will be at His Second Coming.

Please, forgive my jesting. I certainly don't want to ruin anyone's worship experience and this certainly isn't the only chorus that could stand a little lyrical tweaking. Besides, although I am a little dubious about the song's timeline, there *will* be an army that will ride with Jesus on His triumphal return. I want to ride with the Lord then and I want to ride with Him now. Maybe that is what the song is trying to convey in the first place; but, as usual, I have a different take on riding with the Lord now.

When I was a boy, I spent most Saturday mornings helping my mother clean house. This was usually followed by a weekly shopping trip into town. Occasionally, if my father had not already gone to work before I had gotten up, he would ask me if I wanted to ride with him. Nine times out of ten I would respond with the same question, "Where are we going?" Riding with my father could be the highlight of the week. We might go to a cool place like the saw shop or even the Caterpillar dealership where they had the huge bulldozers and other heavy machinery. Other times we would go into deep woods where he had to look at some timber (if you haven't guessed, my father was a logger among other things). There were all sorts of neat places we might be headed, but the best part was there would usually be a treat or snack somewhere along the way.

We might drop by the little country grocery called Five Points where I could get a Mountain Dew or a Chocolate Soldier to drink; or maybe we would end up at Aarons Grocery, another country store, where I could get a Sprite and possibly some Hot Fries. That alone would normally be enough incentive to ride with my father, but I almost always asked the question for one specific reason: sometimes the trip could be more like a lowlight than a highlight.

110

Sometimes, my father's errands didn't involve fun stuff at all. There were times when more work was involved like loading trash into the back of his truck, or perhaps it was simply a trip to talk to someone about business. The trip with my father would be fine; but nothing is more tortuous on a kid than having to sit quietly while adults talk about business, or worse, politics. It would sound like Charlie Brown's teacher, "Wonk, wha wha wha wonk." Hence, the question, "Where are we going?"

My father was equally consistent. The response was always the same: "It doesn't matter where we're going; do you want to ride with *me*?" Man! My father was an expert with the parental psychology. He started by laying that guilt trip on me should I dare entertain the thought of not spending time with my father. At the same time, he would tantalize me, knowing I was deathly afraid of missing something. It was the double whammy that I could rarely resist, and few times did I ever decline to ride. Looking back, I wish I had gone every time. I still don't know everything I missed, but I do know I missed time with my father.

Time we missed with loved ones can never be regained, and that is not just an earthly principle. It works the same way when it comes to our Heavenly Father. Time we miss with Him is time that is lost and, frankly, wasted. He wants to spend time with us so much that He gave His Son as a sacrifice to afford us complete access to His throne. Through His Son, He also invited us to ride with Him. Only He calls it abiding instead of riding. John 15:4-8 - *4 Abide in me, and I in you. As the branch cannot bear fruit of itself, except it abide in the vine; no more can ye, except ye abide in me. 5 I am the vine, ye are the branches: He that abideth*

111

in me, and I in him, the same bringeth forth much fruit: for without me ye can do nothing. 6 If a man abide not in me, he is cast forth as a branch, and is withered; and men gather them, and cast them into the fire, and they are burned. 7 If ye abide in me, and my words abide in you, ye shall ask what ye will, and it shall be done unto you. 8 Herein is my Father glorified, that ye bear much fruit; so shall ye be my disciples. (KJV)

Isn't it amazing that the King of all Glory not only adopts us as His children, but desires to spend intimate time with us? We aren't just orphans He pities and takes in off the streets. He lavishes His love on us, call us His own, and desires to spend time with us, abide with us, ride with us. In fact, it is probably better to describe the process as God riding with us, rather than us riding with Him. When we accept Christ as our Lord and Savior, He comes to live inside of us and we become the temple of the Holy Spirit (I Cor. 6:19). We're sort of like those semi-truck chapels you see parked at the truck stops; we become tiny mobile churches on wheels (or feet).

Abide with the Father and He will abide with you. By doing so, we can be assured that we will ride with Him later. 1 John 2:28 – *And now, little children, abide in him; that, when he shall appear, we may have confidence, and not be ashamed before him at his coming.* Abiding or riding, don't pass up the Father's offer.

CHAPTER 23

A PRICE TO BE PAID

The internet is a wonderful thing. You can send messages around the world in a matter of seconds. You can get headlines from news, weather, and sports current to the minute and you can research just about any topic you can think of, without ever leaving your chair. *And* the best part of all----you know it's all 100% accurate because it's "on the internet". (Do I even need to bother saying that was a joke?) Of course, there are some drawbacks to the internet. It can be impersonal. It makes us more connected, yet simultaneously keeps us from personal interaction. There is a *lot* of misinformation (and other trash) out there; and then there is the biggie, the most insidious bane to mankind ever known-------*SPAM.*

Most of the time, I think I have more e-mail in my junk box than in my regular in box. If you use the internet at all, you have most likely been annoyed by spam---unsolicited, often commercial, mass mailings. Included in this are all the forwards Aunt Martha sends you of every cute kitten picture, health food remedy, and political satire she can find. On the other hand, we all have those people who send us the "good stuff". (Obviously, if I am on your e-mail list, I am to be numbered among those people.) Those are the people who don't inundate us with their junk mail, but are discriminate in their forwarding practices. Whenever you see their name pop up, you think, "This ought to be good." And in most cases it is. You get a laugh, some valuable information, or a heartwarming reflection.

Fortunately, I have some of "those people" who send me interesting forwards from time to time to time to time to…..I'm just kidding. I get some really good forwards; and around every 4th of July, there is one that always seems to circulate. I usually get it at least a couple of times and sometimes more, but I never get tired of it. You have probably seen it yourself. It is a list of the signers of the Declaration of Independence that records what many of them had to sacrifice by taking a stand in the American Revolution. I won't include it here, but the summation is that every one of them had to make a sacrifice of some sort. Moreover, some gave everything----lands, fortunes, sons, and their own lives.

If you have never heard it said before, hear it now------ *FREEDOM ISN'T FREE!* The independence we enjoy today in this incredible country was and is paid for by the blood, sweat, and tears of countless patriots. It doesn't cost you a dime to vote, to worship as you choose, or to stand on the street corner and speak your mind; but somebody gave everything they held dear to earn or maintain those rights and many others for you. Make no mistake. Your freedom was bought and paid for at great price. I don't know how that makes you feel, but when I think about it I have fireworks go off in my heart like New York Harbor on the 4th

114

of July.

Sometimes, when I pause to think about the sacrifices so many made, I have to wonder what those valiant patriots would think of what we have become. Would they smile with pride and hold their heads up high thinking, "It was worth it." Or would we see strong, courageous men and women reduced to tears? All I know is that I may enjoy a gift of freedom that cost me nothing, but I still have an obligation to those who bought and paid for it. I love the last line Tom Hank's character delivers to Private Ryan in the movie, "Saving Private Ryan". With his dying breath he says, "Earn this. Earn this." In the movie, Private Ryan lived the rest of his life trying to be worthy of the sacrifice that was made for him. Wow. If Hollywood can grasp the concept, don't you think maybe we should too?

Of course, as Christians, we have more than a patriotism that drives us. We have been given the ultimate freedom through Christ-------freedom from sin and death bought and paid for by His precious blood. If you have never heard it said before, hear it now----*SALVATION ISN'T FREE.....IT'S FREE TO US.* It cost us nothing to accept the free gift of salvation, but it cost the sinless Messiah his life to provide it. Think about who you are and where you have been. Now, consider that the perfect Son of God gave His life for you. Has there ever been a higher price paid for anything?? And the beauty of it all is even if we could afford the price (impossible), we still couldn't buy salvation. It can only be received as a gift.

I have some more news for you. Salvation is free----your Christian walk is not. I know, I know, we can't get to heaven on works. Well, brother/sister, you ain't getting to heaven without 'em either. James 2:17 tells us that "….faith without works is dead…"

And, from what I understand, dead stuff doesn't make it to heaven. The point is we don't "earn" our salvation but like Private Ryan we have an obligation to live our lives in a manner worthy of the sacrifice made for us. Obviously, we will never be worthy; but that doesn't mean we aren't obligated and it doesn't mean we don't try.

Let's look at the price we have to pay in our Christian walk another way. Suppose I gave you a brand new car of your choice---let's say a corvette. I tell you that I have paid the invoice, tax, tag, and title. Would it cost you anything? Well, no, the gift itself would be absolutely free, wouldn't it? You didn't earn it and you didn't pay the price. But is keeping that gift going to cost you anything? You had better believe it. You have to buy gas, oil, and even tires eventually. And before you even move it, you will have to purchase insurance. I don't even want to think about what that is going to cost you. If you drive it too fast, that will cost you; and if the engine needs repair, that is going to cost you too. Are you getting the picture?

Jesus himself talks about a cost. Luke 14:28 *"Suppose one of you wants to build a tower. Will he not first sit down and estimate the cost to see if he has enough money to complete it?"* The disciples understood the parable; but if they didn't, they certainly would as they walked out their faith. Our founding fathers had nothing on the disciples. If you want to study a who's who list of people who paid a price, then study the fates of the disciples. There are literally thousands of examples from the Bible and time since of people who have paid a price for their faith. Many of those paid with their lives. Many today do the same. No, you don't hear about it on the evening news; and it's not happening at the mall across town. But it is happening.

Ironically, it wasn't a martyr's story that started me thinking of these things. It was a few verses in Acts 17 about a man named Jason. The story is about Paul and Silas escaping from Thessalonica and all we read about Jason is that he was arrested because the officials couldn't find Paul and Silas at his house. Contrast that with our freedoms today. Can you imagine the police breaking down your door, searching your house, and then announcing, "We couldn't find any drugs here. Come with us, you're under arrest." But apparently the officials were angry because Paul and Silas were supposed to be there; and since they couldn't arrest them, anybody associated with them would do.

That was pretty much it. They got booked, fingerprinted, and yelled at a little bit and then they were turned loose. Oh yeah, there was that one little thing in v.9 *"Then they made Jason and the others post bond and let them go."* That got my attention for some reason. They had to pay a price to be released. They had to pay a price because they had chosen to be kind and hospitable to the missionaries. They had to pay a price because they believed in a Way that not everyone would accept. They had to pay a price.

I guess if that is the only price that Jason ever had to pay for his faith, then he probably would have considered himself most fortunate. Maybe. Or maybe he felt like David who said in effect, "I won't offer anything to God that doesn't cost me something." (2Samuel 24:24) I don't know what other prices Jason had to pay, but I know he had to pay something. There is always a price to be paid. Hopefully, you won't be called on to lay down your life for your faith. Hopefully, you won't suffer severe persecution; but rest assured----you will be called on to pay some kind of price. Nothing of value is free. There is always a price to be paid.

CHAPTER 24

CALLING OCCUPANTS

What do you do with the mail you receive in your mailbox addressed to "Occupant"? I throw mine in the floorboard of my vehicle where, on good days, it is transferred to the trash can when I return home. Rarely do we give "Occupant" mail a second look. Why is that? There are various reasons I suppose, but the primary motivation is that we know that the mail was not addressed to us. If a letter has our name and address attached to it we know that the sender meant for it to get into our hands specifically. Mail to an occupant is directed to whoever happens to be opening the mailbox at the time.

There is a difference between occupancy and residency. Occupancy is temporary in nature. Residency has a more permanent status. When we take residency in a place we plan on being there a while. This was made painfully clear to me during a recent move when I discovered how entrenched I had become in my home. I never knew I was such a pack rat or that a couple could accumulate so much "stuff". It isn't just the furniture and pots and pans you have to worry about. There are pictures on the walls, knick knacks, lamps, ladders and mowers and things you accumulate to maintain your castle. And then there are the plants and lawn furniture. The list is seemingly endless, especially when you start to load all that "stuff" onto a truck or trailer. Residents set up camp for the long haul.

Contrast that with occupancy. You can occupy an apartment, a motel room, or a seat at the theater. They all entail varied lengths of occupancy, but the idea is you probably aren't going to be at any of those places permanently. We occupy wherever we happen to be at the time. In fact, you are occupying that space in front of this book right now. With a few exceptions, we have very little attachment to the places we occupy. Again, this is because they are designed to be temporary. We normally don't have anything of extreme value in places we occupy. That is reserved for our residency. Our treasures are in our homes, the place we intend to be long term.

That is why we are supposed to "store up treasures in heaven". We don't want to trust our spiritual treasures to a place we are only passing through. We want them to be protected in the place we will be eternally. Matthew 6:19, 20 -- *19 "Do not store up for yourselves treasures on earth, where moth and rust destroy, and where thieves break in and steal. 20 But store up for yourselves treasures in heaven, where moth and rust do not destroy, and where thieves do not break in and steal."*
It's just like the safes you find in some motel rooms. They are designed to be a safe place to store valuables, but few people use them. We either keep the valuables on our person or leave them at home in the first place. Nothing gives the

feeling of security like home. However, for Christians, this is not our home.

As Christians we should definitely get the feeling of occupancy because we do not belong here. We are aliens in this world who are just passing through. Inside each of us, even if we don't understand it, is a longing to be somewhere else. We will never be truly at home until we actually get home. "The final resting place" is a term sometimes used to reference interment into a cemetery plot, but the grave is not our final resting place (thankfully----a 6' hole isn't much to look forward to!). The grave is the gateway *to* our final resting place. The grave is the doorway home. II Corinthians 5:1-4 - *1 Now we know that if the earthly tent we live in is destroyed, we have a building from God, an eternal house in heaven, not built by human hands. 2 Meanwhile we groan, longing to be clothed with our heavenly dwelling, 3 because when we are clothed, we will not be found naked. 4 For while we are in this tent, we groan and are burdened, because we do not wish to be unclothed but to be clothed with our heavenly dwelling, so that what is mortal may be swallowed up by life.*

Equipped with this understanding, some of us approach our Christian walks as if it's just some kind of investment strategy. "If I can just manage my assets and protect my treasures, I can move into my mansion on Hallelujah Way some day with a pretty impressive portfolio." Not exactly. You see there is a little more to this occupancy thing than meets the eye. We don't just pass through this world without any responsibilities. It's kind of like that apartment or motel room you "occupy" for a short period of time. There is a reason they get your driver's license number and social security number and blood type and all the other information they need. They want to be able to track you down if you cause damage. You are responsible for your time of occupancy and they want you to leave the things just the way you found them. Spiritually speaking we are also responsible for our time of occupancy, but God wants us to leave things much different than the way we found them.

The instructions we are given are found in a parable in Luke chapter 19. A nobleman gives his servants money and instructs them to invest it during his absence. Luke 19:13 - *13 So he called ten of his servants and gave them ten minas. 'Put this money to work,' he said, 'until I come back.'* Other versions read "Occupy until I come". This is the only time in Scripture that this particular form of the Greek word for occupy occurs. It means "to carry on business" or more specifically "to carry on the business of a banker or trader". It is clear that the good news we have been given is a spiritual commodity and that we should be actively "trading" it, not hoarding it like a greedy gold digger.

In the American economic system, we have such a wonderful analogy of this in Wall Street. Are we like the guys down in the pits of the stock exchange; ticker tape (tracts) flying everywhere as we try to move our commodity (the good news), furiously working until the closing bell (the final trumpet)? Or are we like the fat cats practicing insider trading in some smoky back room? You know many have gone to jail for insider trading, the practice of keeping vital information private and using it for one's own gain. This is one thing that God shares in common with the world. He also takes a dim view of "insider trading". Matthew 10:8 - *Heal the sick, raise the dead, cleanse those who have leprosy, drive out demons. Freely you have received, freely give.*

One day, we will hear Gabriel's trumpet version of "Calling Occupants". (I hope it's better than that cheesy version The Carpenter's did in the 80's) At that time, those of us who have made our residence in God's eternal kingdom will go home for the first time and no longer be counted as aliens or occupants. We will be residents of that heavenly City where God is the light. Don't worry about forwarding my mail.

CHAPTER 25

SUCH A TIME AS THIS

We are in a wonderful time in history. Technological advances help us travel faster, communicate more easily, live longer, and, in general, lead better lives than ever before. Occasionally, we hear people opine about the "good ol' days", but I'm guessing not one of those who are quick to give their opinions about yesterday's virtues would be as quick to give up their air conditioners or indoor plumbing. Granted, not all the changes are for the better. Saggy pants have served no redeeming purpose to date and I'm fairly certain the same can be said about multiple body piercings.

Of course, all this is said tongue in cheek. (I can do that because I don't have the multiple piercings.) I do understand that there are serious issues facing our society today. Morality seems to continually spiral downward, but that has always been the opinion of those who oppose evil. The fact remains that for every evil, grace does much more abound; and all in all, there are a lot of great things happening in this era of history in which God has chosen to plant us.

Who am I trying to convince? Well, myself, actually. I

don't know if it is because my parents were a little older than the parents of my peers or if it is because my siblings are so much older than I am, but I always thought I was born too late. I don't know if I really long for the "good ol' days"; it's just that I thought I belonged in them. As Toby Keith would say, "I shoulda been a cowboy." If only they had air conditioning and indoor plumbing back then.

I suppose that most people have those kinds of feelings occasionally. Men are particularly notorious for slipping off into those delusions of grandeur when watching an adventure flick with knights or gladiators or cowboys. What we often fail to realize is that we *are* born to be heroes. Only we weren't born for some medieval fantasy. We were born for such a time as this.

Ironically, that line doesn't come from a story about a man, but from a Biblical account of a young lady---an extraordinarily heroic young lady. Esther was a Jewish girl who became the queen of the Persian Empire. God gave her favor with the Persian king; and through her position, she was able to save the Jewish people from complete destruction. Her story comprises the book of Esther in the Old Testament; and since we will only hit a few highlights here, you should take time to read the entire story again.

The name Esther means "star" and Esther rose to prominence like a shooting star, while possessing the beauty of a Hollywood star. She fit the bill of the typical heroine that would star in an action movie---beautiful, courageous, pressed into service. No wonder there is a book in the Bible dedicated to her story. Then again, if you look a little closer at the book, you will find that there is another character who appears in more verses than Esther and whose name is mentioned even more than the queen's. This character is Mordecai, Esther's uncle, and he was quite the hero as well.

However, these were two heroes who had striking differences. Mordecai's name means "little man". He wasn't the tall, dark, and handsome leading man you would cast as the hero of your action story. (At least we're pretty sure he wasn't tall---who knows about the dark and handsome part?) Esther was tentative, but Mordecai was matter of fact. Esther was thrust to center stage, while initially, Mordecai worked behind the scenes.

Heroes come in all shapes and sizes and they play all kind of roles, but they are all necessary. The movie "Braveheart" would have been pretty bland without Mel Gibson's portrayal of William Wallace thundering at his army with painted face, and it would have been pretty boring if he had gone out to battle the English by himself. Every member of that band of men was a hero, but only one was on center stage. Does that make the others less important? Hardly.

There is one more character we need to mention. Every action story needs a villain and the book of Esther has a perfect one in Haman. Haman's name means "magnificent" and he was the perfect golden child---the good looking glory hound who everybody (except Mordecai) looked up to and admired. Like Esther, his star was on the rise; but unlike Esther, he craved it and lusted after it. It was Haman, who in an effort to get back at Mordecai, initiated the edict that threatened the survival of the Jewish race. How's that for a villain? He felt snubbed by Mordecai, so instead of getting back at just him, he decided he would wipe out his whole race. That certainly wasn't "magnificent".

It was at this time that Mordecai spurred Esther into action with this warning and admonition. Esther 4:14 - *"For if you remain silent at this time, relief and deliverance for the Jews will arise from another place, but you and your father's family will perish. And who knows but that you have come to royal position for such a time as this?"* We know that Esther responded in courageous fashion and saved her people, but can you see how Mordecai deserves a little of the credit as well? Naturally, neither Esther nor Mordecai were seeking notoriety. They simply saw an urgent need and did their part to meet it. If they had childhood dreams of saving the day, those dreams probably didn't even occur to them when they faced this crisis. Yet, that is exactly what they did. They saved the day.

We may never be called on to play a part in such a dramatic story. Sometimes, we may think that our mundane existence is pointless; but that is wrong thinking. Who knows but that we have been placed here for such a time as this? We play our bit part daily and we never see all the cameras rolling, but we mustn't become discouraged and question our role. God is an even better director than Spielberg and He has written every one of us into His script. Jeremiah 29:11 - *"'For I know the plans I have for you,' declares the Lord, 'plans to prosper you and not to harm you, plans to give you hope and a future.'"* Maybe we will be thrust to center stage and maybe we won't; but one day, God will reveal to us how our performance has impacted the grand story He is weaving in such a time as this.

CHAPTER 26

THERE IS A LIGHTHOUSE

When I was a child, I was a little, tiny, hardly worth mentioning, bit of a spoiled brat. (As my brothers and sister would happily attest to) Unfortunately, as an adult, I can still act a little spoiled at times. (As my wife would happily attest to) As adults, we aspire to the virtue of self-sacrifice; but that fruit is often cultivated by the lessons of denial we learn as children. I will never forget the disappointment of my first great denial.

The third pastor of the small church I grew up in was a fascinating brother named Gerald Johnson. He probably possessed many fascinating traits, but I call him fascinating for one reason---he could complete a chalk drawing in the time it took to play a gospel song. In the early 70's, before multi-media presentations, chalk drawings accented with black light were a popular illustrative tool. (You've come a long way, baby!) Our pastor would set up an easel on stage, play a song or have someone sing one, and by the end of it, he would have completed a drawing that matched the theme of the song. Usually, he would flip on a black light at the close of the song for dramatic effect. For a young boy who lived in the time of four television channels, that was fascinating.

The best part of all this was that the drawings were usually given to one of the children in the congregation. I always wanted to get one, but never more than the night Pastor Johnson drew a lighthouse. Ronnie Hinson, a southern gospel artist, had written an instant classic called "The Lighthouse"; and as someone sang that beautiful song in the background, the pastor worked rapidly with his chalk. The singer began to crescendo, *"....then my mind goes back to that stormy night, when just in time I saw the light"* and Pastor Johnson flipped on the black light to reveal the most beautiful lighthouse I had ever seen. The black light made the chalk luminescent and the light in the lighthouse seemed to actually glow. This had to be the night when he would call my name, when I would be the one to receive that awesome picture.

Of course, you know that *wasn't* the night. In fact, I don't recall ever receiving one of those drawings. I did learn those lessons of denial, though. I discovered from that and many other disappointments, you don't always get what you want. I did gain something else from the experience. Whether from my admiration of that drawing or my love for Ronnie Hinson's song I am not certain, but since that time I have had a great affinity for lighthouses. At the risk of overusing the word, they fascinate me.

Lighthouses come in all shapes and sizes, and most come with interesting stories. Some are made of brick or stone, while others are constructed of steel or wood. Some are still functional, but many have become obsolete. Yet, they still stand stoically as if to say, "Don't worry. If you need me, I'll still be here to guide you". I love lighthouses for their history, for their beauty, and because of those enduring lyrics. "If it wasn't for the Lighthouse, where would this ship be?"

Whenever I see a lighthouse, I automatically think of our lighthouse, Jesus. That's why I have several pictures and replicas of lighthouses in our home. I love to be reminded of how "he has shone his light around me". We know that Jesus is the light of the world (John 8:12 -- *When Jesus spoke again to the people, he said, "I am the light of the world. Whoever follows me will never walk in darkness, but will have the light of life."*); but what a beautiful word picture of also being that lighthouse, that symbol of safety that helps us navigate the troubled seas and avoid the rocks of sin.

His mercy and grace extends even farther than being that light and lighthouse for us; He has also made *us* the light of the world. Matthew 5:14-16 -- *14 "You are the light of the world. A city on a hill cannot be hidden. 15 Neither do people light a lamp and put it under a bowl. Instead they put it on its stand, and it gives light to everyone in the house. 16 In the same way, let your light shine before men, that they may see your good deeds and praise your Father in heaven."* We are that lighthouse on a hillside as well; but how can we and Jesus be the light of the world at the same time?

One answer is found in John 9:5 -- *"While I am in the world, I am the light of the world."* When Jesus ascended, He did not take the light with Him; He left us to be His lights. Beyond that, if Jesus lives in us, then His light continually shines *through* us. When people see a difference in our lives, it is His light shining through our clay vessels. Do you know how a lighthouse works? A source of light, usually called a "lamp", shines through a series of lens and is magnified and intensified. That's what Jesus wants to do through us. Through the lens of our lives, He wants to be magnified to the world; to those who are attempting to navigate those troubled seas.

Think again about the "lamp" in the lighthouse. If Jesus is the Word (John 1:1), and the Word is a lamp to our path (Psalm 119:105), then it is easy to see how the lighthouse fits the message of Christ. He *is* our Lighthouse, but we may be the lighthouse he uses for others. Jesus has given us a special mission to be His lights until He returns. Make sure you are a clear lens that He can shine through. Some ship in danger may be looking for your light.

CHAPTER 27

WHO IN HELL ARE YOU?

Once, a friend of mine, a Christian comedian, graciously invited me to spend the day with him when he emceed an outdoor Fourth of July celebration. This included hanging out back stage with him and the participating bands and actually sitting on the stage during some of the performances. That was a lot of fun, but what I really enjoyed were the "green rooms"--- air conditioned RV's where the artists could relax which were stocked with all kinds of food and drinks. The artists had badges (I did not) which authorized their presence in these areas backstage; so as long as I was with my friend I could go anywhere he did.

However, during one of the lulls when he couldn't break away, I decided to wander over to the green room by myself. I was met at the door by a guard who wanted to see my pass and I quickly realized that my good looks and charm were not going to gain me access to the goodies. I learned that as good as my reputation might be, there are times when knowing and, in this case, being with the right person is necessary.

There are certain portions of Scripture that even those who don't profess Christianity tend to put into practice. One of those is Proverbs 22:1 - "*A good name is more desirable than great riches; to be esteemed is better than silver or gold.*" The majority of people are highly concerned with their reputation. Most of us want to be of good reputation; but others think, if they can't be well thought of, they would settle for being.....well, thought of.

Hollywood stars often complain about the unceasing clamoring of the press, but they also know that the absence of the cameras can mean death to their careers. Fame, after all, is defined as being well known. Even children who aren't getting positive attention will act out in an effort to get any kind of attention. It seems the desire to be known knows no age barrier.

As Christians, we desire to be known in heaven; but we understand that it is more than an aspiration---it is a necessity. If our name is not found in the Lamb's Book of Life, we won't suffer anonymity; we will suffer abolition. Nothing is more important than being known in heaven; but once that is secured, wouldn't it also be great to be known in hell? I can hear it now, "He has finally gone off the deep end. Known in hell---who ever heard of such a thing?"

Well, for starters, Jesus was (and is) known in hell. He had to silence the demons when He cast them out to keep them from identifying Him. "That doesn't count. He was *JESUS*. Of course, the demons were going to know Jesus." This is true. Of course that doesn't speak well of the Pharisees, but that's another subject altogether. Still, I submit that every believer who has not been content to sit on the sideline, but rather chose to be active in their faith, has some sort of name recognition in the corridors of hell. (I don't know if hell actually has corridors, but it sounds ominous anyway.)

My absolute, all time favorite example of this is found in Acts 19: 13-16 - "*13 Some Jews who went around driving out evil spirits tried to invoke the name of the Lord Jesus over those who were demon-possessed. They would say, "In the name of Jesus, whom Paul preaches, I command you to come out." 14 Seven sons of Sceva, a Jewish chief priest, were doing this. 15 One day the evil spirit answered them, "Jesus I know, and I know about Paul, but who are you?" 16 Then the man who had the evil spirit jumped on them and overpowered them all. He gave them such a beating that they ran out of the house naked and bleeding.* For all you who thought it impossible to *literally* get your pants beaten off--- think again. The seven sons of Sceva were truly beaten naked or, as we like to say back home, "they toted a whuppin!"

Now that sounds like a fate I wouldn't wish on anybody. I might pay to see it, but I wouldn't wish it on anyone. Yet, if there was ever a crew that got what they deserved, it was Sceva's boys. They were imposters. The term we use today is "posers", but no matter what you call them, the seven sons of Sceva were trying to step into a reputation that wasn't theirs. That was their first mistake. The second mistake was their choice of occupations to masquerade. You can pose as an expert fisherman, doorman, or finger painter, but there are a few areas where you just don't want to fake it. Lion tamer comes to mind. Skydiver is another, and you definitely don't want to fake it as an exorcist.

The first clue that something is amiss is that all seven brothers show up at the possessed man's house. Why do you think all seven went? I am guessing that as priest's sons, they at least had an inkling that messing around with demonic spirits would be dangerous. I'm imagining a conversation something like this.

"That Paul guy sure has it going on with this 'casting out the demons' bit. Hey, Bobby, why don't you go down to that demoniac's house and cast out that demon like Paul does?"
"I'm not going down there by myself. Why don't you go?"
"I'm not going, either. How about you, Billy?"
"I'll go if you go."
"Now there's an idea. Why don't we all go? There's seven of us and only one of him."
And then came the famous last words.
"What's the worst that could happen?"

Another clue that things were going to go bad was the old "yeah, what he said" approach which the sons took to casting out demons. "In the name of Jesus, *whom Paul preaches*, I command you to come out." You would think if you were going to invoke someone's name, you would at least pretend to know him. In any case, a better charade would have done Sceva's sons little good, because the demon knew they had no connection to the power of Jesus' name. "Jesus I know, and Paul I know, but who in the round world are you?" (JHA Enhanced Version)

You can almost see the big "uh oh" look in the boys' eyes right before the beating commences. I love to laugh at this story, but does it hit a little too close to home? Are there times when we too are "posers", professing the name of someone we've heard preached, but really don't know. Perhaps we know Christ, but our resume is not one that would garner attention at the church picnic, much less in hell. Don't be satisfied with anonymity or mediocrity. Make some waves on the lake of fire. Sure, it may bring a little heat, but greater is He that is in you than he that is in the world...or hell.

CHAPTER 28

DEAD OR ALIVE

I was talking with a new friend from south Georgia; and as south Georgia men are prone to do, we started swapping snake stories. Anyone who has spent any time in the country probably has some kind of snake story. It's a story of a close call with a poisonous snake or a fright caused by a harmless rat snake; but in every part of the nation you can find country folks (and sometimes city folks) who have a snake story. However, it's hard to imagine any part of the nation producing better snake stories than the deep South.

The climate of the South accommodates more varieties of snakes for longer periods of time than any other region of the country. In addition, every poisonous snake the nation has to offer can be found in the South and the best snake stories usually involve the poisonous ones. That element of danger just makes the story better.

However, before you jump in and tell your snake story, you have to understand that there is an art involved. Hopefully you have more than one anecdote, because you don't want to lead with your best story. You want to build up to a grand finale. You have to remember that everyone has a snake story (particularly in the deep South), so you need to start slowly and make sure you tell your tales with an air of nonchalance. Nothing is worse than boasting about your best friend catching a 5' rattlesnake with a 12" stick, only to find that someone in your audience has a brother who caught a 6' rattler with his bare hands. It makes you feel like you've just shown Steve Irwin a slide show of your trip to the Everglades.

As my new friend and I exchanged accounts, we cagily tested each other's experience and spun the yarns we had told countless times. I thought I had him with the one about the guy who killed the 4 ½ footer with an 8" crescent wrench, but he got me with a questionable story about a couple that picked up a dead snake which released the baby snakes it had swallowed into their car. I say questionable, but you can only question someone's story in your mind. One of the unwritten rules of snake story telling is that all accounts are beyond dispute. If your friend knows someone who knows someone who killed a cottonmouth with their teeth, then that's the way it happened. (Fortunately, I haven't faced that one yet. Who could top that???)

Somewhere in the midst of our tall tales about the things we have seen snakes do long after they were supposed to be dead, I commented, "Snakes can sure live a long time after they're dead." I know that isn't exactly a brilliant statement (or grammatically correct), but I was caught up in the moment. Snakes have the unusual and yes, creepy ability to keep moving and writhing for long periods of time after they are dead. There is a scientific explanation of nerves or muscles or something, but the fact remains that they appear

138

to be alive when you know they are dead. As the statement of brilliance escaped my lips, I immediately thought, "You know, people can do the same thing."

You may be familiar with the term "dead man walking". It commonly refers to a prisoner who has received a death sentence and is awaiting execution. His fate has been determined and death is imminent, but he is caught in limbo. He is still alive, but he has no future. He draws breath, but he is as good as dead. In essence, he has become a "dead" man long before his execution.

Jesus was actually the first one to use the idea of dead men walking, but he phrased it a little differently. He called the Pharisees "white washed tombs full of dead men's bones". Matthew 23:27 - *"Woe to you, teachers of the law and Pharisees, you hypocrites! You are like whitewashed tombs, which look beautiful on the outside but on the inside are full of dead men's bones and everything unclean."* Jesus was referring to the wickedness and hypocrisy that the Pharisees kept hidden from view as their spiritual death. He always sees things that the rest of us miss…and he also interprets them differently.

Matthew 9:24 tells of the ruler's daughter who had died - *he said, "Go away. The girl is not dead but asleep." But they laughed at him.* The people laughed at Jesus because it was obvious to the human eye that the girl was dead and He called her alive. Maybe the Pharisees laughed as well when they, who were alive, were called dead. The nerve of Jesus to insinuate that *they* were dead. They were the life of the party….well of the synagogue anyway. Who was Jesus to say that *they* were dead on the inside? Well, it just so happens that He was the ultimate authority, then as well as now. He is the one who passes ultimate judgment.

It doesn't matter what the world thinks. If they think we are the picture of health, we might be at death's door; and if they think we are beyond hope, we quite possibly might be at the threshold of a miracle. It doesn't even matter what we think. We may fool ourselves into ignoring the signs of our spiritual demise; but God sees all, knows all, and judges all, righteously and divinely.

In truth, all created beings are alive or dead; not just in the physical sense that we all can discern, but in the spiritual sense that only God can truly discern. The good news is it is really simple to ensure our spiritual life. All we have to do is die. Die to live? What could that mean? Simply put, it means we die *to* our sins so we don't die *in* our sins. Just like Christ was crucified and resurrected, our old nature is crucified and a new creation is resurrected in its place. Because of this, we no longer look upon ourselves or each other as the world would view us.

Paul puts it like this in 2nd Corinthians 5:16, 17 - *So from now on we regard no one from a worldly point of view. Though we once regarded Christ in this way, we do so no longer. 17 Therefore, if anyone is in Christ, he is a new creation; the old has gone, the new has come!*

Though there may not be a visible physical change, dying to our old life makes us spiritually alive in God's eyes. Then we become "live" men (women, boys, girls) walking. That is the most important label we can wear, because dead man walking is a terrible tag to bear in the physical realm; but in

the spiritual realm it is catastrophic. You are
wanted....ALIVE.

CHAPTER 29

AS IT IS IN HEAVEN

Several years ago, as a co-manager of a building supply store, I had the privilege of instructing two manager trainees. My job was to train them according to company policies and prepare them for eventual promotion. Alike in some ways, the two were vastly different in most others. They were approximately the same age and both were athletic, but that was about where the similarities ended. One was dark, the other was blond. One was shy, the other outgoing. One was a natural salesman, the other was not. One had a tremendous work ethic and the other a tremendous ability to avoid work. However, I did discover the second fellow was not scared of work as I found him lying down and sleeping right beside it one day.

Both guys were likable young men; but with one I developed a mutual respect, and to this day he remains like a second son to me. I must admit that a large part of my early affection for this particular young man lay in his desire to please me. He took great pains in learning my particular likes and dislikes in regards to our work load, and he always would do things the way I wanted them done. His parents had taught him well how to respect authority and to give honest effort in his work; so training him was not only easy, it was a pleasure.

I must also admit that I am not the easiest person for which to work. I am obsessive about how I want things done and I most assuredly possess too many pet peeves and peculiarities. More importantly, I am of the mind that a thing worth doing is worth doing right; and I have made many a task be redone in the name of that credo. With that in mind, the trainee after my own heart (as I like to refer to him) once told some of the other workers, "Fellas, I don't know why you don't do it like he (that would be me, otherwise known as Simon Legree) wants it done in the first place. You know he's going to make you redo it if you don't." It made perfect sense to me.

I didn't just like this young man because he was a good worker (although that didn't hurt). I liked him because the work ethic was in him. You can teach someone how to work, and you can teach someone your ways of doing things; but a work ethic takes a while to develop, and that's if the person wants to learn. Some do the job, but they do it begrudgingly: you can almost see the obligation written on their face as they strain under the system. Others find satisfaction in a job well done. It's just in them.

I remember watching the two trainees one day from a window at the store's front counter. The first rounded the corner of the front dock in his usual quick pace. Noticing one of the four trash cans we had out front was slightly out of place, he stopped, centered the can, and gave it a ¼ turn so the adhesive logo we had placed on its side would face the parking lot. *That's my boy. Nice job on that. That's been bugging me all morning.* On the opposite end of the dock, the other trainee transferred a delivery into our special order room. Another delivery had already been stacked beside the room; and as the trainee walked back toward the entrance, a gust of wind caught one of the doors and blew it to the ground in front of him. Startled as it crashed at his feet, he deftly jumped over the door and continued to walk back to the front counter. *Certainly, he is going to pick that up......Certainly, he is not going to leave that door on the ground.* But he certainly did. He was laughing as he entered the store. "Did you see that door?" he asked. "It almost hit me; I had to jump over it." "I sure did," I replied. "Nice move, by the way. Hey, you don't mind going back out there and picking that thing up for me, do you?" Sometimes it's in them and sometimes it's not.

These two young men came to mind as I listened to a worship chorus based on the Lord's Prayer. The line "let it be done in the earth as it is in Heaven" kept being repeated over and over again. As I sang the line in unison with the choir, the question popped into my mind: how *is* the Father's will done in Heaven? I began to realize that Jesus might not have simply been talking about the Father getting his way here on earth like He does in heaven. After all, we know He *is* going to get His way. It's not like we're going to hinder that, even if we tried. Then I remembered those two trainees. It wasn't what they did that impressed me; it was the manner in which they did it. Perhaps, we should be doing the Father's will here on earth the way they do His will in Heaven; but how do they do it in Heaven?

The only one we know who has observed heavenly operations first hand is Jesus, so let's see if we can pick up some clues from His words. First, it is apparent that the Father's will has priority. Matthew 26:39 - *Going a little farther, he fell with his face to the ground and prayed, "My Father, if it is possible, may this cup be taken from me. Yet not as I will, but as you will."* Through the example of Christ, we see that the Father's will supersedes our objections no matter how valid they may seem.

Secondly, obedience to the Father's will is ultimately an act of love. John 14:23, 24 - *23 Jesus replied, "If anyone loves me, he will obey my teaching. My Father will love him, and we will come to him and make our home with him. 24 He who does not love me will not obey my teaching. These words you hear are not my own; they belong to the Father who sent me.* When we obey, we demonstrate our love and are also brought into relationship with Christ. Matthew 12:50 - *For whoever does the will of my Father in heaven is my brother and sister and mother."*

Finally, harmony with the Father perfects the completion of His will. John 5:19 - *Jesus gave them this answer: "I tell you the truth, the Son can do nothing by himself; he can do only what he sees his Father doing, because whatever the Father does the Son also does.* This goal of harmony is what Paul encouraged in Phil. 2:1,2 - *If you have any encouragement from being united with Christ, if any comfort from his love, if any fellowship with the Spirit, if any tenderness and compassion, 2 then make my joy complete by being like-minded, having the same love, being one in spirit and purpose.*

145

I am convinced that the fulfillment of the Father's will lies in attitude as well as action; but in either case, His will must come to fruition in our lives if we are to enter His kingdom. Matthew 7:21 - "*Not everyone who says to me, 'Lord, Lord,' will enter the kingdom of heaven, but only he who does the will of my Father who is in heaven.* Search your own heart and examine your actions and motives. May this be your prayer today: Thy will be done in my life....as it is in Heaven.

CHAPTER 30

WHEN I AM STRONG, THEN I AM WEAK

Have you ever received a compliment and wondered what the person was *really* trying to say? "That color looks really good on you." *Do the other colors look bad on me??? Have I been wearing unflattering colors lately???* "That was very thoughtful of you." *Am I not normally thoughtful??? Have I been rude recently???* "You smell nice today." *OH NO! Do I even want to go there?!?!*

Sometimes it's difficult to interpret the true meaning of a person's words, but sometimes it's as easy as pie. When a state trooper asks you for your license and registration, you don't hand him your fishing license and a warranty card from a recent appliance purchase. You know exactly what he's asking. The same was true when you were a child and your father said, "I'm going to knock you into the middle of next week if you open your mouth again!" You understood the hyperbole, but you also knew your best chance of staying in the current time/space continuum was to keep your mouth shut.

The premise was simple-----if one statement of fact had a certain result, then the inverse of the statement would naturally produce the opposite result. So in our example if opening your mouth meant time travel, then keeping it closed would obviously mean staying safely put in the current week. If playing with a BB gun meant someone would lose an eye, then not playing with one meant everyone grew up with both their peepers. This was the rationale that guided us safely through our childhood. Of course, as adults, we want to slap some fancy moniker on it like "cause and effect"; but in most cases, it still serves us just as well as it did in our youth.

Sometimes, however, we get so caught up in the original statement that we give little thought to the inverse. I believe such is the case when Paul talks about his thorn in the flesh in 2 Corinthians 12. He points out that the power of Christ is perfected in us through our weakness; and then he caps it off in verse 10 with the ultimate statement of contradiction, ".....for when I am weak, then I am strong." We can hardly fathom Paul's assertion. How can that be??? Eventually it sinks in that our strength is miniscule (if that) to Christ and that only when we acknowledge this will He exhibit His awesome power on our behalf. By that time, it seldom occurs to us to explore the inverse of Paul's statement. If I am strong when I am weak, then could it be that I am weak when I am strong? And I would like to ask more specifically is there vulnerability in our strength which catches us unaware?

I love the obscure stories in the Bible, and the one that probably fascinates me the most is found in 1 Kings 13. It tells the story of a man of God who travels to Bethel by the instruction of the Lord to confront the wicked king, Jeroboam. The Lord uses the man to perform miracles including the withering and subsequent healing of Jeroboam's hand. The man follows God's instructions to the letter including specific directions to neither eat nor drink in Bethel and to leave the town by a different road than the one on which he entered. Everything is going great until an old prophet in town hears about the events and goes after the man to persuade him to return to Bethel to dine with him at his home.

The prophet finds the man of God sitting under an oak tree and extends his invitation. At first the man refuses, citing God's instructions to him; but the prophet lies to him telling him that the Lord had *commanded* the prophet to go after the man of God. At this point, the man of God relented and returned to Bethel disobeying the specific instructions that God had given him. During the meal, the prophet began to prophesy (this time in truth) and told the man of God, "Because you have disobeyed the command of the Lord........your body shall not come to the grave of you fathers." Essentially he was saying, "You ain't going to make it home, brother." And that is exactly what happened. When the man left the prophet's house that evening, he was killed by a lion and his body was thrown on the road.

This story never ceases to amaze me. Used, and used mightily by God in the morning---dead because of disobedience in the evening. How could that happen? Well, first I see a grave warning to be diligent in our obedience to God. But secondly, I see the distinct possibility that somebody riding high on the euphoria of being used by God, quite possibly never considered the idea that in such a moment of strength he would be a prime target for the enemy. When are our eyes most keenly focused on God? Is it not when we are in the middle of battle or service? Or at low point when we are in desperate need? When are we most likely to take our eyes off of God? Could it be when things are great and we are satisfied? Or immediately following some awesome victory when we pause to reflect on what God just did through US? When we look *back* at what was just accomplished?

Consider where the old prophet found the man of God---- under an oak tree. I don't know why he was there. Maybe he was tired. Maybe it was hot and he needed relief from the afternoon sun. But maybe, just maybe, he was resting on his laurels a bit. Perhaps he spied a nice comfortable spot to reflect on how God had just used him and wanted to ponder what new ministry God had in store for his obvious talents. I don't know what he was doing, but I do know that at some point he stopped operating in God's strength and started operating in his own. And I also know at that point he became instantly weak.

Don't be deceived. Satan will attack us at any point of life, but he knows that because of our prideful natures we are susceptible to distraction immediately following the high points more often than the low points. This chapter could easily have been titled, "Nice Job.....Look Out!", for our greatest achievements often bring our greatest tests. How often have we heard of someone who seemed to be on top of the world taking a harsh tumble? "How could they let that happen?" we ask. Well, isn't it true in our own lives? Haven't you done the same thing on perhaps a smaller scale?

On Sunday morning the pastor delivers a great message and you feel the power of God. Then, before you can get out of the parking lot, your spouse catches you off guard with something trivial and you snap back in a very un-Godly fashion. Sound familiar? Well, that wasn't your spouse catching you off guard; that was Satan. (And no, I did not just call your spouse, Satan.)

Satan even tried the same trick on Jesus after his 40 day fast recorded in Matthew 4 and Luke 4. Some would say that Satan attacked Jesus after his fast because he was in a weakened state, but I am not sure that is entirely accurate. He was hungry and thirsty in *body*, but His *spirit* was stronger than ever. The only chance Satan had of knocking Him off was to appeal to His vanity. If he could make Jesus believe that he had finally arrived and didn't really need the Father any longer then he would have the ultimate conquest. If you don't believe it, look at the temptations. 1) Perform a miracle and supply your own need. Be your own resource. 2) Go to the pinnacle and show your authority. Let everyone see your power. 3) Rule the kingdoms of the world. Take your throne. Do those sound like temptations for a person of weakness? No, they were temptations to a person who had seen and felt the awesome power of God; and they failed because Jesus never took His eyes off of His true goal and His true source. That is how we will overcome. Remember to be sober and vigilant because our adversary, the devil, is roaming around like a lion seeking someone to devour. (1 Peter 5:8) Don't be afraid and don't shy away from great exploits in the name of the Father. Just be wise and wary. And the next time someone says "Nice Job!"........Look Out!

CHAPTER 31

THE NECESSARY THINGS

I love the story about the hippie, the smartest man in the world, and the President of the United States all riding in an airplane together. (This *is* a joke so suspend critical thinking and accept the fact that the President was riding coach with the other two.) Unfortunately, the plane's engines failed and the plane began to plummet. Being heroic men, the three made sure that everyone including the crew received a parachute and was able to evacuate the plane. When it came time for the three men to make their jump, they made a horrifying discovery: there were only two parachutes left. Immediately, each man began to make the case why he should get one of the remaining chutes. "I am the leader of the free world," said the President. "I have vital secrets and information that protect our nation. I have to be saved for the safety of millions." Who could argue with that? The hippie responded with, "Well, I don't have all that responsibility, but I do have a dog named Boo that needs me to take care of him and I *could* be important one day." The smartest man in the world said, "This is ridiculous. I am the smartest man in the world, and the knowledge I possess can impact everyone on the planet. I have to go." And with that, he grabbed one of the parachutes and jumped from the falling plane. The President looked at the hippie in dismay. In his most presidential demeanor, he told the young man, "You know, I have lived a great life. I am going to give you the chance to do what I have done. Go home to Boo and make your mark on the world." The hippie coolly replied, "It's okay, Mr. Prez; we can both go." "The smartest man in the world just jumped out of the plane with my knapsack!"

Have you ever felt like that? In all of your infinite wisdom, have you ever made the absolute best choice and then later found it was the absolute worst choice? All your deliberation and careful thought became worthless as you frantically searched every angle of your choice, much like the smart man clawing at that knapsack looking for a ripcord. Like him, you desperately looked for a way to release that saving canopy; but it never happened. We've all been there. It apparently wasn't life or death (or I wouldn't be writing and you wouldn't be reading), but it certainly seemed like it when we were in the midst of it.

It is through these experiences and observing the examples of others that we learn what the necessary things are. There is nothing like freefalling over planet Earth to make you realize that, for that situation, a parachute is a necessity. Books and pillows may make the trip more comfortable, but they are quickly cast aside if the plane starts to fall. The folks on the Titanic suffered for the lack of the necessary things. The fine china and opulent furnishings made for an elegant experience—until the iceberg was struck. Then there was only one thing necessary -- lifeboats, and there weren't enough of them to go around. 1,517 people would have traded everything they owned for that one necessary thing.

153

Again, our decisions probably aren't so dramatic; but then
again, maybe they are. We are careful with our personal
physical safety and the safety of our loved ones. We take
great pains everyday to make sure our families are protected.
We guard against predators, intruders, and forces of nature.
These are the necessary things; but do we follow the same
diligence in spiritual matters---prayer, meditation, the
reading of God's Word, and fellowship with other believers.
These things are even greater necessities.

As important as they are, we still have the tendency to
downplay them or even overlook them totally. Even in the
presence of Jesus, we can be blind to the necessary things.
How could that happen? Maybe it's not as hard as we might
think. Luke 10:38-42 - *38 Now as they went on their way,
Jesus entered a village. And a woman named Martha
welcomed him into her house. 39 And she had a sister called
Mary, who sat at the Lord's feet and listened to his teaching.
40 But Martha was distracted with much serving. And she
went up to him and said, Lord, do you not care that my sister
has left me to serve alone? Tell her then to help me. 41 But
the Lord answered her, Martha, Martha, you are anxious
and troubled about many things, 42 but one thing is
necessary. Mary has chosen the good portion, which will not
be taken away from her.*

Martha was so busy running all *around* Jesus that she didn't
take time to be *with* Jesus. Was there anything wrong with
preparing the meal? No, definitely not (and all us fat boys
said, "Amen!"). She wasn't doing a bad thing; she was
doing a good thing. Actually, she was doing a good thing for
Jesus; but the good things can be what trip us up the most.

154

"Good things become bad things when they keep us from the best things."

Jesus wasn't angry with Martha. In fact, you can almost hear the tenderness in His voice as you read the words "Martha, Martha..." He wanted Martha to grasp the truth that Mary had already come to understand: choosing the eternal over the temporal is always the best choice. Sitting at the feet of Jesus always takes precedence over serving at His hand. It is what equips us to be able to serve. Rest assured that if we are listening at His feet, He will let us know when it is time to rise and serve at His hand.

Don't fall into the same trap that Martha did. The good things you do in the name of Jesus are important and appreciated, but they are not always what are necessary. Jesus wasn't angry with Martha and He isn't angry with you. He just wants to spend more time with you. He wants you to choose the necessary things. He wants you to choose Him. It sounds like a great choice to me.

Made in the USA
Charleston, SC
02 June 2014